3/17

SAVAGE SALADS

First published in 2016 in the UK by Frances Lincoln
Limited, a subsidiary of Quarto Publishing Group UK

Published in the United States of America by
Gibbs Smith
PO Box 667
Layton, UT 84041

1.800.835.4993 orders
www.gibbs-smith.com

Designed by Ashleigh Bowring

ISBN 978-1-4236-4492-7
Library of Congress Control Number: 2016945730

Printed and bound in China

21 20 19 18 17   5 4 3 2 1

SAVAGE SALADS

FIERCE FLAVORS
FILLING POWER-UPS

DAVIDE DEL GATTO AND
KRISTINA GUSTAFSSON

GIBBS SMITH
TO ENRICH AND INSPIRE HUMANKIND

CONTENTS

AUTUMN

WINTER 131

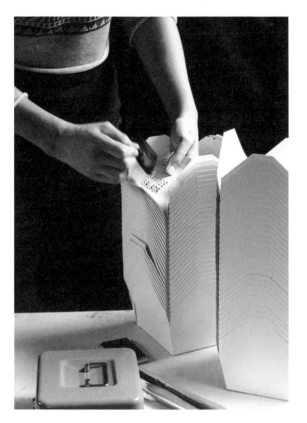

WHAT IS A "SAVAGE SALADS" SALAD?

The Savage Salads team believes that salads should taste amazing, look beautiful, and leave you full.

Salads were once thought of as something boring served on the side of your main meal, a half-hearted attempt at being "healthy". They used to be (and occasionally still are!) a sad mix of iceberg lettuce, cucumber, a few slices of tasteless tomato, and, if you're lucky, a sprinkling of canned sweetcorn.

Thankfully, things have come a long way. Restaurants are now serving incredible and inventive salads, shops are stocking exciting, international ingredients, and there's been a great shift in our attitude toward eating fresh, wholesome and healthy foods.

We're all open to international influences from the Middle East, South America, Scandinavia, and beyond, meaning canned sweetcorn should be the last thing you reach for. Instead, get stuck into salads mixed with chickpeas, olives, black beans; and top your nourishing dishes with pickled herring, serrano ham, or a skewer of lamb.

In our experience, though, there's still a lingering notion that salads can't be truly satisfying and can't deliver the protein of a "real" meal. It's the Savage Salads mission to quash that idea and prove that salads can be enticing, wholesome, filling, and packed with protein. To do this, we sell proper salads from our London stall—keeping people full from lunch until dinner—and we've written this book packed with *real* salad meals.

And what is the difference between a salad and a "savage salads" salad? Interesting flavor combinations, being creative with the many and varied grains that are available, and not being afraid to add red meat, chicken, fish, cheese, nuts, and seeds to turn a salad into the main event of the meal. This book isn't for crash-dieters and vegetarians: we want to inspire people to eat well because good food is delicious— any health benefits are an additional bonus.

We've also kept the ingredients and methods simple, because everyone should feel confident and comfortable throwing our recipes together—from our five-minute salads to dinner-worthy dishes, these are recipes that are easy to prepare and fun to eat and share.

The book is arranged by season, because at the heart of our food is our belief that the best meals come from the freshest ingredients. Salads used to be for summer, stews for winter. Not any more. A winter salad of nourishing grains, enlivened here and there with bright segments of clementine or sharp, sweet pomegranate seeds, is every bit as satisfying on a cold day as pie and mash.

It also means the recipes are suited to people's needs and cravings throughout the year. In the summer chapter, you'll find light and refreshing salads using a lot of raw ingredients; in winter, cooked root veg and comforting combinations demonstrate that salads can be a pleasure all year round.

Seasonal ingredients, exciting flavors, irresistibly good: this is healthy food the Savage Salads way.

WHO ARE SAVAGE SALADS?

Davide and I [Kristina] are Savage Salads. At the crack of dawn each day, we head to our industrial-size kitchen to prepare fresh, seasonal, and tasty salads. We make enough to feed the several hundred people that queue at our stall in Soho in London every lunchtime (come rain, shine, frost, or even gales!), all of them eager to buy one of our delicious packed lunches. Into every box go four salads—each one is full of punchy flavors and satisfying textures—and these are topped with one delicious protein (meat, fish, or cheese) to help keep people going all afternoon.

We have a lot of gym-junkie fans who can't get enough of Savage Salads—our protein-rich and vitamin-packed boxes are perfect fuel pre- or post-gym—but it's definitely not just health enthusiasts who come to us. People tell us they're bored of limp supermarket salads and the same old sandwiches, so a lot of office workers love the variation we offer, and then there are the people who are just into good food and exciting flavors, something Davide and I brought to the stall through our heritage.

Davide was born in Naples in Italy where food was central to a good life. In his early childhood, he moved to Tuscany with his family, but his parents continued to be dedicated to traditional Neapolitan cuisine. Davide grew up with food. He loved helping his mother and grandmother as they prepared the family meals; and he learned that seasonal, fresh ingredients (and minimal interference) often make the best dishes.

He moved to London in 2001 hoping to improve his English, and soon started working in restaurants and developing his passion for food and international cuisines.

Following most culinary career paths, Davide first took a job as a kitchen porter, but quickly worked his way up to head chef.

I grew up miles away from Davide in the culinarily creative country of Sweden. My parents took great pride in using locally sourced ingredients and vegetables from our own garden in their cooking. Like many other Swedes, we would go out in the forest and pick mushrooms and berries, go fishing for dinner, and plant potatoes and other root veg that we'd dig up to use in our family meals.

I moved to Dublin in my late teens and began working in restaurants, before hopping over to London to do more of the same. In the last decade I've worked in kitchens, as well as front of house, and have become even more enthusiastic about good food and healthy eating.

Davide and I met in 2011 while working at the same London restaurant and we quickly realized we had a shared dream of owning our own food business. We were both keen to experiment with the flavors we'd grown up with, and also to encourage people to eat more healthily. So among the stalls selling buttermilk fried chicken and smoked ribs on chips, we set up Savage Salads as a beacon of healthy eating—and not just for vegetarians. This was food for people who liked to fill up and feel nourished, and eat something a little more exciting than a jacket potato or soggy sandwich.

Now we're looking to take Savage Salads beyond the streets of Soho and into the homes of the health-conscious (and taste-conscious) with these beautiful recipes. It's simple, it's salad, but with a "savage" twist.

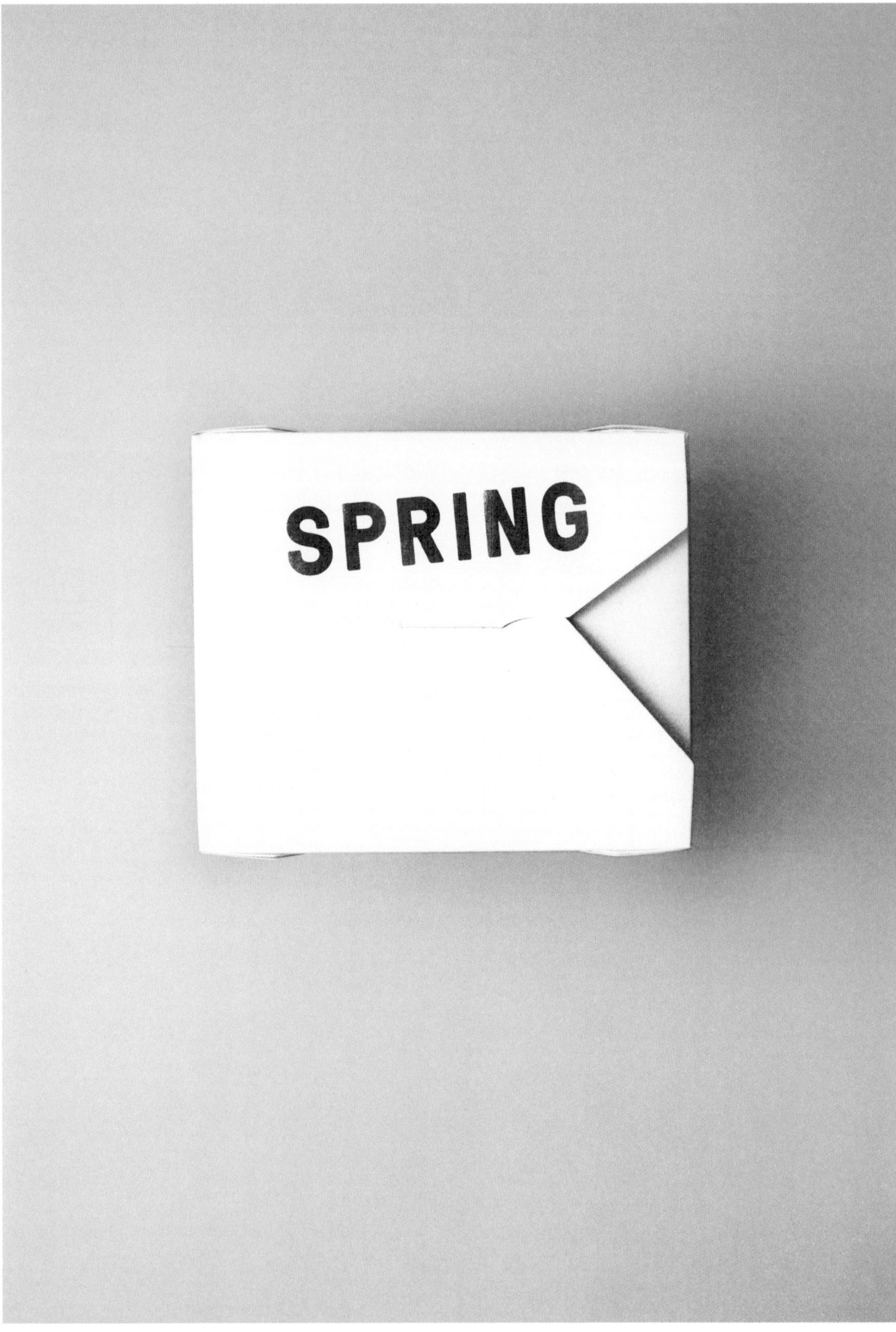
SPRING

SPRING

Spring is the season for light, fresh salads. Everything around us is slowly coming to life again: the trees and flowers are blossoming, and the very best bright and crunchy veg (think peas, radishes and asparagus) are ready to be picked.

Ingredients are so sweet and plentiful at this time of year that you needn't go overboard with cooking and preparation—using totally raw ingredients, or quickly blanching them, means you'll enjoy all the flavors and colors of this season, and get all the nutritional benefits too.

But to make sure your salads are more than a bit of veg on a plate and, most importantly, to ensure they're satisfying, think about which vegetable combinations will give you the most dynamic dish, which grain would fit the bill, and which meat or fish best complements the salad. It's about experimenting with flavors—something that's far easier to do when you don't have to worry about complex cooking methods.

Some recipes in this chapter are super-light (such as the spring greens salad on page 31, which has an added hazelnut crunch), while others would make filling dinner options (go to page 54 for red mullet with amaranth seeds, fennel, and fava beans). They all share the spirit of the season, and will all leave you with a spring in your step.

FIVE MINUTE SALAD

sprouting broccoli

feta

grapefruit

watercress

slivered almonds

mint

Blanch 7 ounces broccoli in boiling salted water for 3 minutes. Drain and cool under cold running water. Break 7 ounces feta into small pieces. Peel 1 grapefruit and use a small knife to cut the segments from inside the white membrane, cutting from the outside to the center. Combine with 7 ounces watercress and ¼ cup slivered almonds. For a dressing, whisk together 1 tablespoon white wine vinegar, 10 mint leaves, a pinch of salt, and 2 tablespoons extra virgin olive oil and use to dress the salad.

ASPARAGUS, POACHED EGG YOLK, RADISH, PECORINO, SPECK

Spring is the perfect time to eat delicate asparagus. There are many ways to use these tender stalks but we love them grilled or steamed in salads. In this recipe we steam the asparagus so it's still crunchy— the soft poached egg yolk acts almost as a dressing once you break it over the finished dish, and the speck and pecorino add a salty finish. This dish is great for brunch, as well as lunch.

- 5½ oz Italian speck, rind removed
- 3½ oz pecorino
- 12 asparagus spears
- 4 large eggs
- 1 tbsp vegetable oil
- 5½ oz red radishes
- 1 tbsp white wine vinegar
- 2 tbsp extra virgin olive oil
- salt and freshly ground black pepper

Serves 4

Make sure the speck and pecorino are both at room temperature, as this will allow the full flavors of these key ingredients to be enjoyed at their best.

Trim about 1–2 inches off the bottom of the asparagus (this should be where the stalks would naturally snap if bent in half), then place them in a steamer set over a pan of boiling water and cook for about 4 minutes, or until just tender.

Meanwhile, to make the poached egg yolk, bring a small pan of water to a gentle boil. Separate the eggs, then very carefully slide a spoon under the yolks, one by one. Gently put them into the pan of water and cook for about 2 minutes, or until the outside of the yolk is firm (the center should still be soft). Remove them carefully from the water with a slotted spoon and leave in a warm place while you make the salad.

Heat the vegetable oil in a pan over medium heat until hot. Chop the speck into small ¼-inch dice and put in the hot pan and fry for 1 to 2 minutes, until crisp. Remove and put the speck into a large bowl. Finely slice the radishes (a Japanese mandolin is very useful for this) and add to the bowl. Roughly chop the asparagus and add to the bowl too.

Whisk the vinegar with the olive oil and dress the salad. Season to taste and arrange on serving plates. Finely shave the pecorino over the top and add a warm egg yolk.

GRILLED RUMP STEAK, ASIAN RADISH, CARROTS, WATERCRESS, SESAME SEEDS, SESAME OIL

When you crave a good steak, the rump cut is an inexpensive and tasty choice. Beef can be quite a heavy meat, but we've lightened this dish up by serving it with a crunchy and super-healthy salad. It's a great choice for a low-carb but filling meal. The sesame oil and seeds give the dish an Asian flavor.

- 4 rump steaks
  (9–10½ oz each)
- olive oil, for cooking
- salt and freshly ground
  black pepper
- 2 large carrots
- 1 Asian radish
- 5½ oz watercress
- ¼ cup sesame seeds
- juice of 1 lemon
- splash of sesame oil

Serves 4

DRESSING SUGGESTION
Watercress mayonnaise p 177

Heat a nonstick skillet until smoking hot. Season the steaks with salt, black pepper, and a drizzle of olive oil, then place the steaks in the pan and cook on one side (without moving them) until brown.

Turn the steaks over and cook for another 2 minutes. Remove the pan from the heat and leave the steaks to rest.

Peel the carrots and Asian radish, then use a mandolin to cut them into julienne strips. Place them in a bowl and add the watercress, sesame seeds, lemon juice, and sesame oil, then mix together.

Arrange the salad on serving plates. Slice the beef and place on top of the salad.

GRILLED LEMON SOLE, ARUGULA, KALAMATA OLIVES, SPELT, GARLIC CROUTONS, CHERRY TOMATOES

Lemon sole is a fantastically tasty and beautifully delicate fish. The best way to cook it is to grill it on the bone so that the fish remains moist and flaky. Once the fish is cooked, meat should come off the bone very easily and you can add chunks of it to the salad. Since the fish is quite light, we've added spelt and croutons to make this dish more substantial. If you prefer it to be gluten free, use quinoa in place of the bread and spelt.

- Scant 1 cup/7 oz pearled spelt grains
- 7 oz stale white bread
- 4 garlic cloves, crushed
- extra virgin olive oil
- 2 whole lemon soles, about 14 oz each skin on
- grated zest and juice of 1 lemon
- 1 bunch of thyme
- 7 oz cherry tomatoes
- 5½ oz kalamata olives
- 3½ oz arugula
- salt and freshly ground black pepper

Serves 4

Preheat the oven to 300°F.

If the packet states you need to soak the pearled spelt grains, add them to a bowl of water and leave overnight. The next day, drain and set aside. You can also buy spelt that doesn't need pre-soaking.

Cut the bread into equal-sized cubes, then put them on a baking tray. Add a few splashes of olive oil, sprinkle over the crushed garlic, and a pinch of salt. Place the tray in the middle of the hot oven and bake for 30 minutes, or until the bread is slightly golden and crunchy. Remove and set aside.

Preheat the grill to maximum and line a baking tray with parchment paper.

Put the fish on the baking tray and season with salt, pepper, grated lemon zest (reserve the juice for later), and a few sprigs of thyme. Drizzle some olive oil over the top of the fish and place under the hot grill for about 10 to 15 minutes, or until the fish is cooked through. Remove, allow to cool, then cut into chunks.

Continued overleaf

DRESSING SUGGESTION

Citrus dressing p 174

Meanwhile, drain the soaked spelt grains (if soaking) and put the spelt in a pot with about 1¼ cups water. Place the pot over medium heat, cover with a lid, and simmer for 15 to 20 minutes, or until the water has evaporated and the spelt is soft. (Alternatively, follow the instructions on the packet.)

Prepare the tomato salad by cutting the cherry tomatoes in half and placing in a large bowl. Roughly chop the olives and remove the pits if they are not already pitted, and place in the bowl with the tomatoes. Add the arugula, croutons, and spelt grains. Drizzle the lemon juice over the salad and add a few pinches of salt and a couple of glugs of extra virgin olive oil.

Mix the salad, then divide among serving plates. Add the chunks of lemon sole. Serve with a couple of lemon slices on the side.

GREEN BEANS, PEAS, FAVA BEANS, STRING BEANS, HAZELNUTS, SOY SAUCE

This is another Asian-inspired salad made from a mix of the best vegetables that spring has to offer. The beans and peas only need a couple of minutes in boiling water to soften them up slightly—you still want to keep that crunch. The vivid green colors are a dazzling celebration of spring.

- 3½ oz shelled fresh peas
- 3½ oz fine green beans
- 3½ oz string beans
- 3½ oz shelled fava beans
- 1 tbsp soy sauce
- juice of 1 lemon
- 1 tsp toasted sesame oil
- ⅓ cup/1¾ oz hazelnuts, roughly crushed

Serves 4

For every 3½ oz fresh peas you will need about 10½ oz peas in the pod—the same applies for the fava beans, if you're using fresh—look to buy three times in weight as what you expect to use, to avoid any shortfall.

Top and tail the green beans and string beans. Using a vegetable peeler or a sharp paring knife, remove the fibrous edges of the string beans from top to bottom.

Blanch the fava beans in a pan of boiling water for 2 to 3 minutes, then remove and cool under cold water. Pop the beans from their cases and set aside. Cut the string beans widthwise quite thinly—no more than ¼ inch. Chop the green beans in half.

Blanch the peas, green beans, and string beans together in a pan of boiling salted water for 3 minutes. Drain and set aside.

Meanwhile, whisk the soy sauce, lemon juice, and sesame oil together in a large bowl. Add the peas, beans, and hazelnuts to the bowl, mix well and serve.

This dish can also be served cold—just refresh all the cooked ingredients in cold water before re-draining.

MUSTARD MARINATED PORK FILLET, COUSCOUS, CARAMELIZED GRAPES, RADICCHIO, CRACKLING, CILANTRO

Fillet is the choicest cut of pork, but it's not pricey. If you cook it properly (using a meat thermometer), it can be delicate and tender, and isn't fatty at all. The couscous base will give a Mediterranean feel to the dish making it fresh and light, while the warm grapes add a juicy touch as soon as you cut into them.

- 2 pork fillets (roughly 1 lb 6 oz in total)
- ½ bunch of thyme
- 4 tbsp grain mustard
- extra virgin olive oil, for cooking
- finely grated zest and juice of 1 lemon
- 5½ oz pork skin
- 2½ cups couscous
- 2 garlic cloves
- 1 bunch of cilantro, leaves only, chopped
- knob of butter
- 7 oz red and white grapes

Continued on page 35

Cut off any excess fat and tissue from the outside of the pork—a little fat is good for cooking, but you want to remove any thin silvery skin from the outside, as this does not break down during cooking. Put the pork in a shallow bowl.

Chop the thyme quite finely and add to the mustard with some salt and pepper, a glug of olive oil, and half of the lemon juice. Pour the marinade over the pork to cover, then place in a sealable plastic food bag and chill in the refrigerator for 2 hours.

Preheat the oven to 300°F. Roll the pork skin and cut into ¼-inch pieces. Place on an oven tray and bake in the oven until crispy.

Put the couscous in a bowl. Chop the garlic finely. Heat a little olive oil in a small skillet over low heat, add the garlic. Cook for 2 to 3 minutes, until softened. Add the garlic to the couscous together with the remaining lemon juice, the zest, and some salt. Work this mixture into the couscous until all the grains are coated. Add a little extra olive oil if it feels too dry. Add the chopped cilantro leaves, then pour boiling water over the couscous, just enough to cover it, then cover with a loose-fitting lid and leave for 20 minutes to soften.

- ½ head radicchio, leaves
  separated (torn in half
  if they are large)
- salt and freshly ground
  black pepper

Serves 4

DRESSING SUGGESTION

Wholegrain mustard
dressing p 170

Heat a pan over low heat. Add a knob of butter and when melted, add the grapes. Cook, stirring every few minutes, for about 8–10 minutes, until they are caramelized.

Preheat the oven to 400°F. Remove the fillets from the bag, getting rid of any excess marinade from them as it will burn in the pan before the pork is cooked.

Heat a little olive oil in a nonstick pan, add the pork. Sear it, rolling it around in the pan until browned all over, before placing in the oven. Cook for 10 to 15 minutes for medium meat, or 20 to 25 minutes for well done. For best results, use a meat thermometer—when the inside of the meat reaches 140°F, the meat is ready. In all cases, remove the pork from the oven when cooked and leave to rest for 5–10 minutes.

Use a fork to fluff up the couscous and separate the grains. Check the seasoning and add more if required.

Arrange the couscous, radicchio, and grapes on serving plates, mixing them up. Slice the pork into medallions about 1 inch thick and arrange on top of the couscous then scatter the crackling over the top. Serve with the wholegrain mustard dressing on p 170.

RICOTTA AND PARMESAN GNUDI, NETTLES, SPINACH, PINE NUTS, RED AMARANTH LEAVES

Gnudi is a Tuscan-style dumpling and it's also the name for the inside of a ravioli. They are usually served boiled or rolled in semolina and then fried until golden—they can be used to top many different salads. Nettles are often used as a medicinal herb but they are also great to cook with: they can be used in pestos, purées, or soups, or just sautéed. The important thing is to wear gloves while picking the nettles and then blanch them to get rid of the sting. Flavor-wise, nettles are quite similar to spinach, but they contain more protein and fiber than your usual leaves. Together with the amaranth, they make this a very earthy dish.

- 1¾ cups/14 oz ricotta
- 1½ cups fine semolina
- ⅓ cup grated parmesan
- 1 tsp grated nutmeg
- 1 large egg yolk
- 1¾ oz nettle leaves
- 14 oz spinach
- 1 tbsp extra virgin olive oil
- ¼ cup pine nuts, toasted
- Scant 1/4 cup/1¾ oz red amaranth
- salt and freshly ground black pepper

Serves 2 to 3

Place the ricotta in a piece of muslin. Gather the corners together and secure them tightly with a rubber band. Put the muslin parcel in a colander or strainer set over a bowl in the refrigerator for 4 to 6 hours. This is to squeeze out some of the liquid from the cheese, so make sure the ball is tightly bound so the liquid drips through.

Spread the semolina out on a large tray. When the ricotta is ready, remove the cheese from the muslin and put in a bowl, then beat in the parmesan, nutmeg and egg yolk. Season to taste with salt and pepper.

Wet your hands a little and dip them in the semolina to stop the ricotta sticking to them. Using a tablespoon and working quickly, scoop out a ball of cheese and roll it around in your hands, then drop it into the semolina and roll it around to cover. Pick it up, roll it in your hands again until the surface is smooth, then drop it back into the semolina and roll it around until it is covered. Repeat with more balls of cheese until all the mixture is used up.

Continued overleaf

When all the balls are made, transfer them to a clean tray and leave them, uncovered, in the refrigerator overnight.

The next day, blanch the nettle leaves in a large pan of boiling water for 30 seconds to remove the sting, then drain and transfer to a nonstick pan over low heat. Add the spinach and the extra virgin olive oil and cook for 1 to 2 minutes, until the spinach has wilted.

Blanch the gnudi, in 2 or 3 batches, in a large pan of boiling water for 2 minutes, or until they float to the surface. Drain.

Divide the warm salad mix among serving plates, and arrange the gnudi on top with the pine nuts and red amaranth leaves. Drizzle with olive oil, or the basil-infused oil on p 178.

SEA BASS, CLAMS, SHRIMP, SEAWEED, CHILLI, GINGER, GARLIC, CUCUMBER

This recipe combines an Italian cooking technique called cartoccio (steam cooking in foil or paper) with Asian flavors. Cooking food this way keeps all the flavors and moisture within the parcel; it's also a very healthy way of cooking as you only need a drizzle of oil.

- 3½ oz fresh ginger root, peeled and finely sliced
- 2 sea bass fillets, about 1½ lb each
- 2 garlic cloves, chopped
- 7 oz clams
- 14 oz shrimp, shelled and deveined
- 1 oz cilantro
- 1 small red chilli, deseeded and finely chopped
- 4 sheets of nori seaweed
- 1 tbsp sesame oil
- 1 lemon, cut in quarters
- scant ½ cup rice wine (mirin)
- 1 cucumber
- salt and freshly ground black pepper

Serves 4

DRESSING SUGGESTION
Ginger and sesame dressing
p 181

Preheat the oven to 400°F.

Place 2 large pieces of foil on the counter and lay the ginger slices on one side of each, then divide all the ingredients, except the sesame oil, lemon, rice wine, and cucumber, between the two.

Place the ingredients in the center of the foil (or you can use strong parchment paper), breaking up the nori into small pieces as you go. Place the fish on top of the shrimp and clams, then season well with salt and pepper and fold the edges of the foil up into a parcel shape.

Before you crunch the edges together, pour in the rice wine and sesame oil (half the amount to each parcel), and add a lemon quarter to each. Now fold the edges together to form a neat parcel allowing some space above the ingredients for steam, as the parcel will puff up. Carefully place the parcels in the hot oven and cook for 15 minutes.

Meanwhile, slice the cucumber into short ribbons and divide among the serving plates.

When ready, remove the foil parcels from the oven and place one on each plate and serve, allowing your guests to open the parcel themselves, mixing the contents with the fresh cucumber.

CHICKPEA GNOCCHI, FENNEL SAUSAGE, PURPLE SPROUTING BROCCOLI, SUN-DRIED TOMATO, GARLIC CRESS

Gnocchi has been one of Davide's favorite things to cook (and eat) since he was a child, and his grandmother taught him the classic Italian recipe with potato and wheat flour. We've swapped the wheat flour with chickpea flour. This adds a more nutty flavor to the gnocchi and is great if you want to avoid gluten.

- 10½ oz luganega sausage
- 4 tbsp olive oil
- 1¼ cups/10 fl oz white wine
- 2 lb mealy potatoes, such as King Edward, unpeeled
- 5 cups/1¼ lb chickpea flour
- ½ cup grated parmesan
- 1 tsp grated nutmeg
- 1 egg
- 10½ oz purple sprouting broccoli
- 7 oz spinach
- finely grated zest and juice of 1 lemon
- 5½ oz sun-dried tomatoes in oil

Continued on page 44

Remove the sausage from the casing, then cut into 3in pieces (or crumble into small pieces).

Heat 1 tablespoon olive oil in a skillet over medium-high heat. Add the sausage, stirring occasionally, and cook for 5 to 8 minutes, until browned all over. Pour in the wine, reduce the heat to a simmer, and cook, turning occasionally for another 15 minutes, until the wine has evaporated. Remove the pan from the heat and leave to cool.

Place the potatoes in a large pan of salted water and bring to a boil. Once boiling, reduce the heat slightly to a gentle boil and cook for 30 to 45 minutes, or until you are able to pierce them easily with a sharp knife. Drain the potatoes and leave until they are cool enough to handle, then peel off the skins.

Put the potatoes into a ricer and press them down on to a clean counter.

Sift the flour on to the potatoes, add a good pinch of salt, the parmesan, and nutmeg, then break the egg into the center. Work all the ingredients together with your hands until they come together and form a ball.

- salt and freshly ground black pepper
- punnet (small box) of garlic cress or ordinary cress, to garnish

Serves 4

Break palm-sized pieces from the ball and roll out into sausage shapes on to the counter. As you roll each one, stretch them out and lengthen them by gently moving your hands away from each other. When finished, the gnocchi lengths should be about ½ inch in diameter.

Using a dough scraper or large knife, cut the gnocchi into roughly ½-inch pieces, flicking the knife up after each cut to stop them sticking to the counter. When all the gnocchi have been made, bring a large pan of salted water to a boil. Add the gnocchi and cook for 2 minutes, or until they float to the surface. Remove from the water with a slotted spoon, drain well and toss in 1 tablespoon olive oil.

Peel the casing off the sausage and discard, then break the meat up into small nuggets. Set aside.

Blanch the broccoli for 2 minutes in a large pan of boiling water, then set aside. Cook the spinach in another pan with 1 tablespoon olive oil until wilted, then add the broccoli and season with salt and pepper and a squeeze of lemon juice.

Roughly chop the sun-dried tomatoes and set aside.

Heat the remaining olive oil in a large heavy-bottom skillet over medium-high heat. Add the gnocchi, in 2 or 3 batches if necessary, and the sausage meat and cook until the gnocchi turns a golden-brown color, then remove and drain on kitchen paper. Place the broccoli and spinach on serving plates, arrange the gnocchi on top, and spoon the sausage meat over that. Sprinkle the tomatoes and garlic cress over and finish by grating the lemon zest over each plate.

CONFIT SALMON, SNOW PEAS, PINK GRAPEFRUIT, GREEN BEANS, POPPY SEEDS

The word confit *is French and means to cook meat slowly in its own fat. This is most commonly used when cooking duck, but it works with other ingredients and in this recipe we use salmon cooked in olive and vegetable oil. This technique is a great way to keep the salmon soft and moist, and the herbs and lemon in the oil really add extra zip to the fish.*

- 2 pink grapefruits
- 4 slices of salmon, about 2 in thick, cut from the thick end, skinned and pin-boned
- 7 oz slender green beans, ends trimmed
- 7 oz snow peas
- sprinkling of poppy seeds
- scant ½ cup extra virgin olive oil
- juice of ½ lemon
- 2 cups/vegetable oil
- salt and freshly ground black pepper

FOR THE CONFIT OIL

- 2 cups olive oil
- 1 bay leaf
- 1 sprig of thyme

Line a small oven dish with parchment paper. To prepare the confit oil, put the non-virgin olive oil in the oven dish with the herbs, garlic, and lemon rind (the oil needs to be deep enough to submerge the salmon portions completely). Cover and set aside at room temperature for 2 hours to allow the flavors to infuse with the oil.

Preheat the oven to 250°F.

Peel the grapefruits with a very sharp paring knife, working from top to bottom, making sure to remove the pith as well as the peel. Remove each segment by slicing either side of the membrane from the outside of the fruit to the inside—you should be left with individual segments with no membrane attached.

Place the salmon fillets (skin side down) into the olive oil and herb mixture, then put the dish into the hot oven and cook for 20 to 25 minutes.

Meanwhile, bring a pan of water to a boil. Add a little salt and the green beans and cook for 3 minutes. Add the snow peas and cook for another 2 minutes then drain. Refresh the beans and snow peas under cold running water and drain again. You can leave them in the colander to drip dry while you prepare the rest of the dish.

Continued on page 49

- 2 garlic cloves, crushed but intact
- grated rind of 1 lemon

Serves 4

DRESSING SUGGESTION

Lemon and dill dressing
p 166

After 20 minutes of cooking, check one of the salmon fillets with a sharp knife by piercing it into the center—the flesh should just be turning from translucent to opaque, like what you would normally see in a medium-rare steak. If the salmon has not reached this stage, return to the oven and cook for another 5 minutes, then check again.

Remove the salmon slices from the hot oil with a pair of kitchen tongs and place them on a metal rack to allow the excess oil to drip off.

Place the drained snow peas and beans into a salad bowl with the grapefruit segments and poppy seeds. Dress with a little extra virgin olive oil and the lemon juice, and season with salt and pepper.

Arrange the salad on serving plates, then place a portion of confit salmon on top of each one and serve. You can flake up the salmon and mix it in if you prefer.

RABBIT AND LEEK TERRINE, GREEN TOMATO CHUTNEY, FRISÉE

Making a terrine from scratch might seem like a long and difficult process, but this is a simple recipe where the ingredients are pre-cooked in one mix (rather than layers) and left to set. It's best to use rabbit legs here, as when you braise them the natural gelatin from the bones will be released helping the terrine to set.

FOR THE CHUTNEY

- ¾ cup packed brown sugar
- ⅔ cup white wine vinegar
- 1 onion, finely chopped
- 1 garlic clove, finely chopped
- 1 thyme sprig
- ½ cup golden raisins
- 1 lb 2 oz green tomatoes
- salt and freshly ground black pepper

FOR THE TERRINE

- 1 tbsp olive oil
- 4 rabbit legs
- 2 carrots, roughly chopped
- 1 onion, roughly chopped
- 1 thyme sprig
- 1 bay leaf
- 2 tbsp/1 oz butter
- 7 oz pancetta, diced

Continued on page 53

First, make the chutney. Heat the sugar and vinegar in a skillet until the sugar completely dissolves and it's bubbling. Add the remaining ingredients, bring to a boil then reduce the heat to a simmer and cook for about 1 hour, or until the chutney is thick. Remove the thyme, season to taste and transfer to a sterilized jar.

To make the terrine, preheat the oven to 350°F and line the sides of a terrine mold (roughly 8 x 2 x 5 inches) with plastic wrap. Fill the terrine mold with water to iron out any creases, then pour out the water and pat dry with a paper towel.

Heat 1 tablespoon olive oil in a skillet and add the rabbit legs, carrots, and onion. Brown for 5 minutes, then transfer to a roasting dish and add the thyme, bay leaf, and enough water to reach halfway up the legs. Cover with foil and braise in the hot oven for 1½ hours, or until the meat is falling off the bone.

Meanwhile, heat a knob of butter in a skillet over medium heat. When melted, add the pancetta, leeks, shallot, and garlic and cook for about 10 minutes, or until most of the fat melts away from the pancetta. Remove from the heat and put into a mixing bowl.

When the rabbit legs are ready, remove the dish from the oven and leave until cool enough to handle.

Remove the legs and pick the meat off the bones, breaking it up into small pieces as you go.

- 2 leeks, cut into circles
- 1 shallot, finely chopped
- 2 garlic cloves, finely chopped
- 3½ oz cornichons
- ¾ oz tarragon, chopped
- salt and freshly ground black pepper

FOR THE FRISÉE

- 1 head of frisée lettuce
- 1 round lettuce
- olive oil
- lemon juice, to taste

Serves 4

Strain the cooking liquid into a pan, discarding the braising vegetables, and cook over high heat for 15 to 20 minutes, until it has reduced by half.

Roughly chop the cornichons and set aside.

Add the reduced liquid, the rabbit, tarragon, and the cornichons to the pancetta and shallot mix. Season to taste, mix well, and spoon into the lined terrine mold. Cover with a rectangular piece of wax paper and place a heavy weight on top so that the mix is pressed down. Leave to set in the refrigerator overnight.

For the frisée, trim the darker, drier tips of the leaves and discard. Cut the round lettuce from the core, rinse under cold running water, and dry, preferably in a salad spinner. Put the frisée in a salad bowl with the leaves from the round lettuce, dress with a little olive oil and lemon juice, season to taste, and serve with a generous spoonful of the cooled chutney and a thick slice of terrine.

RED MULLET, AMARANTH, FENNEL, FAVA BEANS, ALFALFA SPROUTS

If you love quinoa you should definitely give amaranth a try. Amaranth is high in protein and is naturally gluten free. The grilled fennel and fava beans add great flavor to the delicate fish.

- 7 oz amaranth seeds
- 5½ oz fava beans, shelled
- 1 fennel bulb
- 3 oz alfalfa sprouts
- 4 large red mullet fillets
- rock salt
- olive oil
- 1 lemon
- salt and freshly ground black pepper

Serves 4

DRESSING SUGGESTION

Citrus dressing p 174

Put the amaranth in a pot and cover with water. Cook over medium-low heat until the water has disappeared and the amaranth has softened. Remove from the heat and leave to rest for 10 minutes.

The easiest way to shell fava beans is by blanching them in a pan of boiling water for 1 minute, then draining and refreshing under cold running water. Pinch each one between your fingers—the bean will pop out quite easily from the casing.

Heat a skillet over medium heat. Remove the stalks from the fennel bulb and slice very thinly against the grain, removing and discarding cross sections of the root as you go. Add the slices to the hot skillet and toss them around in the pan for 2 minutes, or until they have got some color on them. Remove from the heat and set aside.

Put the cooked amaranth, fava beans, fennel, and alfalfa sprouts together in a large bowl. Tease the sprouts apart with your fingertips if they are clumped together.

Heat a nonstick pan. Season the fish fillets with a generous pinch of rock salt, then drizzle a little olive oil over them and place them skin-side down in the hot pan, in 2 batches if necessary. Cook for 2 minutes, until the edges begin to crisp, then put the pan into the hot oven for another 6 to 8 minutes.

Meanwhile, season the salad ingredients with salt and pepper, drizzle a little extra virgin olive oil on top, squeeze over the juice from half of the lemon, and toss well. Arrange on serving plates and place a fillet on top of each one, skin-side up. Using the remaining half of the lemon, serve with a lemon wedge each.

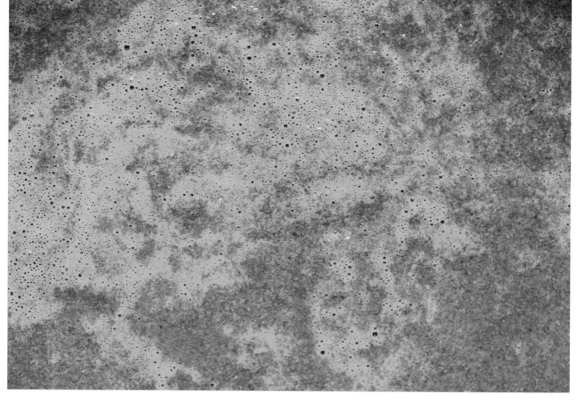

blitzed salad

CHILLED WATERCRESS SOUP

This soup is super-healthy, nutritious, and light. It's the perfect soup for spring, because this is the optimum time to pick and eat watercress. For a creamier version, you can serve with a dollop of crème fraîche on top.

- 2 tbsp olive oil
- 1 small onion, finely chopped
- 1 small mealy potato, such as King Edward, finely diced (optional)
- 14 oz watercress
- sea salt

Serves 4

Heat the olive oil in a pan over low heat. Add the onion and sweat for 2 minutes. Add the potato, if using, and a good pinch of sea salt, then cover with a lid and cook very gently over low heat for 10 minutes.

Add 2 cups water and bring to a boil, then reduce the heat to a simmer and cook for 12 minutes, or until the potatoes are soft.

Transfer the cooked potatoes to a blender. Add the watercress and purée until smooth. Season to taste with sea salt, then pour the mixture into a container with a wide base and leave to cool in the refrigerator before serving.

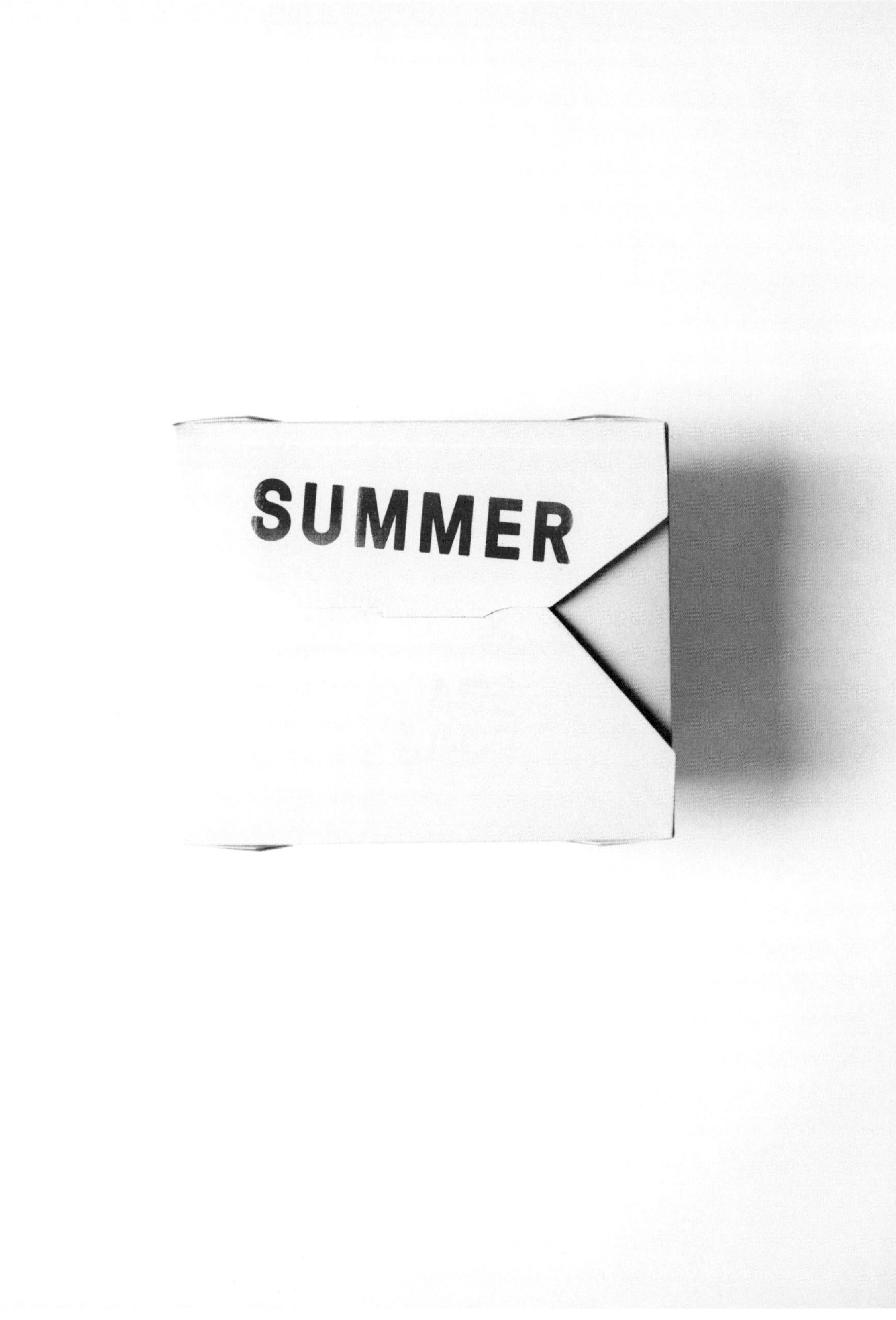
SUMMER

SUMMER

Being street food traders and working
outdoors all year, we absolutely love
it when summer finally comes around.
Not only is it a great time to enjoy
being out in the sun (the market has a
brilliantly busy buzz!), it's also the
best season for salads because the most
exciting, colorful ingredients are at
their peak.

You can head down to your local market
(or even the supermarket) and pick up
ripe, succulent produce bursting with
flavor—look out for cucumbers, zucchinis,
and eggplants, as well juicy summer fruit
from plump peaches to fragrant figs. Or
if you're lucky enough to have a vegetable
patch or allotment, this is the time when
your hard work will really be paying off.

It's a good season to experiment with
sweet elements in your salads, such as
pomegranate or mango—these are ideal for
creating salads that give you a holiday
vibe on a workaday Monday. Look to our
zesty shrimp, zucchini, mango, chilli,
and grilled pita combo on page 78 for
a taste of the exotic. Or wait for the
weekend and treat friends to a backyard
feast of barbecued lamb cutlets, grilled
eggplants, pepper, and mint yogurt (see
page 86).

FIVE MINUTE SALAD

fennel bulb

zucchini

celery

mint

lemon

Remove the core from 1 fennel bulb with a
paring knife and slice as thinly as possible.
Slice 1 zucchini lengthwise into ribbons. Peel
and discard the fibrous skin from 1 celery
stalk and chop into ¼-inch pieces. Combine
with a few mint leaves. For a dressing, add
the juice of ½ lemon, a drizzle of olive oil,
and a pinch of salt.

GRILLED APRICOTS AND PEACHES, COUSCOUS, MINT, SERRANO HAM, PINE NUTS

This is a lovely summer dish that's easy to make. The salty ham really complements the sweetness of the peach and the apricots. When you buy your fruit, pick ones that aren't too soft as they tend to stick to the pan quite easily. We've also chosen to serve this dish with moghrabieh (Lebanese couscous) but you can use any type of pearl or giant couscous.

- ¼ cup/2¼ oz pine nuts
- 1 cup giant couscous
- 8 ripe apricots
- 8 ripe peaches
- vegetable oil, for rubbing
- juice of ½ lemon
- splash of extra virgin olive oil
- splash of balsamic vinegar
- 5½ oz thinly sliced serrano ham
- salt
- mint leaves, to garnish

Serves 4

DRESSING SUGGESTION
Splash of balsamic vinegar

Toast the pine nuts in a nonstick skillet over low heat for 5 to 7 minutes, tossing occasionally, until golden-brown. Remove from the heat and set aside.

Bring to a boil plenty of water in a large pot, with a pinch of salt. Add the couscous and cook for 9 to 10 minutes, until soft. Drain the couscous and rinse under cold running water.

Cut the apricots and peaches into quarters. Put your stove on maximum heat and place a grill pan or griddle on top. Make sure the pan is smoking hot before you start grilling the fruit.

Rub the peaches and apricots with a little bit of vegetable oil to keep them from sticking to the grill. Put the fruit on the grill and leave for about 5 minutes, until they do not stick to the grill any more.

Once all the fruit is grilled and cooled, put it in a bowl together with the couscous and pine nuts. Squeeze in the lemon juice and dress with a splash of extra virgin olive oil and balsamic vinegar. Mix together well.

Place everything on a plate and serve with the sliced serrano ham and fresh mint leaves on top.

BEETROOT AND GIN CURED SALMON, PICKLED CUCUMBER, CRISPY RYE

Cured salmon is a classic in Sweden. The curing process takes quite a bit of time, but the preparation is quick and easy. The beetroot stains the fish beautifully leaving a deep blush around the edges, and the gin adds character.

- 2 fresh beetroot, peeled
- grated zest of 2 lemons
- scant ¼ cup/2 fl oz gin
- 1/2 cup rock salt
- ¼ cup raw brown sugar
- 1 lb 2 oz side of salmon, pin-boned
- 4 slices rye crispbread
- 1 punnet of salad cress

FOR THE PICKLED CUCUMBER

- 1 tsp pickling spice (available ready mixed)
- scant ½ cup white wine vinegar
- 2 tbsp granulated sugar
- 1 tsp chopped dill
- ½ cucumber, very thinly sliced

Serves 4

DRESSING SUGGESTION

Swedish or French mustard

Grate the beetroot into a bowl and add the lemon zest, gin, rock salt, and raw brown sugar. Mix well.

Place the salmon skin-side down on a large piece of plastic wrap and cover the flesh side with the beetroot cure, pressing it into the flesh with the back of a spoon. Wrap the plastic wrap around the fish tightly and leave in the refrigerator for 36 hours.

A couple of hours before you serve the salmon, heat the pickling spices in a small dry pan over medium heat for 5 minutes, or until they smell aromatic.

Add the vinegar, sugar, and a pinch of salt. Stir until the sugar has dissolved. Remove from the heat, stir in scant ¼ cup water, and leave to cool. Once cool, add the chopped dill, sliced cucumber, and a pinch of salt. Leave to stand for an hour or so.

Remove the salmon from the refrigerator and unwrap it. Scrape the beetroot cure carefully from the flesh and discard.

Carefully rinse any remaining cure from the fish under a slow running tap. Be careful not to drench it. Pat dry with kitchen paper and slice very thinly.

Divide the rye crispbread among serving plates, arrange the pickled cucumber on top, then the salmon, and finish with a sprinkle of cress.

RICOTTA AND RAISIN STUFFED ZUCCHINI FLOWERS, WATERCRESS, BLACK SESAME SEEDS

In Italy this is an alternative fritto misto *(fried fish) dish for vegetarians. The trick to making this dish work is getting the batter and the temperature of the oil right. The batter can be made with beer instead of soda water (though soda water is a lighter option). Either way, this might not be the healthiest option in the book, but it's a great little salad and it's truly delicious.*

- ½ cup all-purpose flour
- 2 tbsp cornstarch
- pinch of baking soda
- 1 egg
- scant 1 cup/7 fl oz chilled soda water
- ¼ cup golden raisins
- 1½ cups/12 oz ricotta
- grated zest and half the juice of 1 lemon
- 8 zucchini flowers
- 1 large zucchini
- 1 tbsp vegetable oil, plus extra for deep-frying
- 2 tbsp extra virgin olive oil
- 1 tbsp vegetable oil, plus extra for deep-frying

Continued on page 70

First, make the batter. Sift the flour, cornstarch, and baking soda together. Add a pinch of salt and a twist of pepper. Break the egg into the bowl and add the soda water. Whisk together quite briskly until it is a smooth batter. (Don't worry if a few small lumps remain, this is preferable to overmixing). Cover and leave the batter in the refrigerator while you prepare the rest of the ingredients.

Soak the raisins in a heatproof bowl of freshly boiled water for 10 minutes, then drain and squeeze out any excess water. Put the ricotta into a bowl, add the raisins, lemon zest, a few drops of lemon juice, and salt and pepper to taste, then give everything a good mix.

Cut a cross shape into the base of the zucchini flower where it was originally attached to the zucchini: this will allow it to cook more quickly in the fryer. Carefully prise open the petals of each zucchini flower and spoon in the mixture, being careful not to overfill them. You need to be able to close the flower back up afterwards. Gently twist the ends of the petals together to close them.

Top and tail the large zucchini, cut in half widthwise and then slice each half lengthwise into ribbons. Heat 1 tablespoon vegetable oil in a pan over high heat. Add the zucchini ribbons and stir-fry them very quickly.

- 3¼ oz watercress
- 2 tsp black sesame seeds
- salt and freshly ground black pepper

Serves 4

DRESSING SUGGESTION
Citrus dressing p 174

This should take no more than 2 minutes.

When the ribbons are done and nicely colored, put them into a bowl with the remaining lemon juice and the extra virgin olive oil, then season to taste. Don't worry if the zucchini ribbons are still a little firm, they will soften more as they cool.

Using a deep-fat fryer or a deep saucepan, heat enough vegetable oil for deep-frying to 350°F.

Remove the batter from the refrigerator, give it another quick stir, and dip 2 or 3 zucchini flowers at a time (depending on how many will fit in your fryer). Carefully lower them into the hot oil and deep-fry for 3 to 4 minutes, turning them occasionally. Lift them out with a slotted metal spoon and drain on kitchen paper. Continue until all the flowers are cooked.

Toss the zucchini ribbons together with the watercress and arrange on serving plates with 2 deep-fried zucchini flowers on top of each plate. Sprinkle the sesame seeds over the top, season with salt and pepper, and serve.

MARINATED CHICKEN, ARTICHOKE, GRILLED LEMONS, RED QUINOA

This is the recipe for the chicken we serve at our stall. We always marinate it overnight to make the meat super-tender, but even two hours is enough to absorb the lovely thyme and rosemary flavors.

- 1 small bunch of thyme
- 1 small bunch of rosemary
- 2 lemons
- 6 garlic cloves
- 4 skinless, boneless chicken breasts
- 8 artichokes
- 1½ cups red quinoa
- 7 oz arugula
- extra virgin olive oil
- 3½ oz parmesan
- salt

Serves 4

DRESSING SUGGESTION
Basil and arugula pesto
p 160

Roughly chop the herbs. Grate the zest and juice of one of the lemons (reserve a quarter of this lemon) and crush the garlic cloves with the flat side of a broad, heavy knife. Mix these with the chicken, add a splash of olive oil, and leave covered in the refrigerator for at least 2 hours.

Preheat the oven to 400°F. Trim the woody, outer leaves from the artichokes and cut off the tips from the top leaves. Peel the stems and cut away any excess, leaving about 2 inches. As you work through them, rub lemon juice from the reserved lemon quarter on to the exposed areas.

Put the artichokes into a non-metallic roasting dish with a drizzle of olive oil, cover loosely with parchment paper, and add about scant ½ cup water to the dish. Cook in the hot oven for 20 to 25 minutes.

Cook the chicken breast on the stove in a heavy nonstick pan over low heat for about 20 minutes, turning frequently, until golden-brown and firm to the touch.

Bring the quinoa to a boil in 1¾ cups salted water and when most of the water is absorbed, about 15 minutes, reduce the heat to very low, stir well, cover, and cook for another 5 minutes. Leave to cool slightly in the pan.

Cut the second lemon into quarters lengthwise, drizzle with olive oil, season, and grill for a few minutes on each side on a grill pan until it colors slightly. Leave to cool.

Toss the quinoa, artichokes, arugula, and grilled lemons together. Add a little extra virgin olive oil, check the seasoning, and arrange on plates, shaving parmesan over the top. Slice the cooked chicken quite thickly and place on top.

NDUJA, BURRATA, BURNED EGGPLANTS, SLOW-DRIED CHERRY TOMATOES, BASIL

This dish is a mouthwatering blend of flavors originating from the south of Italy and includes some of our favorite ingredients. The creamy burrata, the spicy nduja, and the sweet slow-roasted cherry tomatoes make a fantastic team. Nduja is a spicy, spreadable pork sausage that's as awesome on a piece of bread as it is in a pasta sauce. When you fry it, it releases a spicy oil which, in this recipe, you can use to drizzle over the finished dish.

- 1 lb 2 oz cherry tomatoes
- rock salt
- 2 eggplants
- ¾ oz basil
- 7 oz nduja sausage
- 2 balls burrata mozzarella
- 1 tsp extra virgin olive oil, plus extra for drizzling
- salt and freshly ground black pepper

Serves 4

Preheat the oven to 210°F and line a large shallow oven tray with parchment paper.

Cut the cherry tomatoes in half along the middle (not through the top where the stalk was)—this allows more of the liquid to be exposed and makes drying more efficient. Arrange them in a single layer on the lined oven tray and season with rock salt and a few twists of black pepper. Cook in the oven for about 2 hours.

Keep checking them; if they are turning dark at the edges turn the heat down 25°F or so. You should see them shrivel and lose most of their weight as the water evaporates. When they are ready, and they have shrunk considerably, remove from the oven and leave to cool.

Wrap the eggplants individually in 2 layers of foil and place in a dry, wide-bottom pan. Cook the eggplants on the stove over high heat with nothing else added to the pan, turning them occasionally. You are aiming to scorch the skins inside the foil while the flesh softens and cooks in the center. Keep turning them until they feel soft and squishy throughout. This will take about 20 minutes.

Continued overleaf

Remove the eggplants from the pan and leave to cool slightly.

Meanwhile, chop the basil quite finely and add to a large bowl with the dried tomatoes. Season with salt and pepper to taste and drizzle a little olive oil over. Set aside.

Slice the nduja into ½-inch circles. Heat the olive oil in a pan over medium-high heat and add the nduja. Cook for about 5 minutes, or until it sizzles and breaks apart.

Spoon the eggplant flesh (leaving behind the skin) on to 4 serving plates. Tear the burrata mozzarella and add a piece to each plate. Scatter the tomatoes around and spoon over the hot nduja, including the juices and oil. Serve straightaway.

GRILLED SHRIMP, ZUCCHINI RIBBONS, MANGO, CHILLI, GRILLED PITA

This was one of the first salads we ever had on our stall. It was an immediate success and helped us realize that people were hungry for Savage Salads-style lunches. Since then we've created many variations of this dish, but this one remains our all-time favorite. It has an exotic twist, it's lovely and light, and it's perfect on a hot summer day.

- 1 large zucchini
- extra virgin olive oil
- 1 mild red chilli, deseeded and finely chopped
- 1 large, ripe mango
- 16 shrimp, peeled, deveined, heads removed and tails still intact
- 4 pita breads (white or wholemeal)
- grated zest and juice of 1 lemon
- salt and freshly ground black pepper

Serves 4

DRESSING SUGGESTION

Coconut yogurt p 181

Preheat a chargrill pan or barbecue.

Top and tail the zucchini and slice lengthwise quite finely. Season with salt and pepper and add a drizzle of olive oil.

Put 3 tablespoons of olive oil into a small saucepan and heat over very low heat. Add the chopped chilli and cook very gently for about 3 minutes. Set aside to allow the oil to infuse with some of the heat of the chilli.

Slice the mango around the pit, remove the skin, and chop roughly. Set aside.

Place the shrimp in a dish, drizzle a little olive oil over them, season with salt and pepper, and place on the hot chargrill or barbecue (you can use skewers if easier). Cook, turning them a couple of times, for 4 to 6 minutes, or until they change color and firm up a little. Remove and cook the zucchini slices in the same way for 3 minutes. Remove the zucchini and place the pitas on the grill to warm up. When warm, roughly chop them into pieces.

Put the zucchini and mango together in a bowl and dress with the warm chilli oil. Season with salt and pepper.

Arrange the salad on serving plates, adding the shrimp on top. Squeeze some lemon juice over, divide the pita pieces among the plates, sprinkle with the lemon zest, and serve.

FIGS, BLUE CHEESE, PECANS, CRACKED WHEAT, ARUGULA

Figs are great dried, made into jams or used in desserts, but you can't beat a fresh fig when it's in its prime. The strong flavor of the blue cheese and the sweet figs go really well together. Any blue cheese works in this recipe, but we recommend a creamy one such as dolcelatte or gorgonzola. The cracked wheat turns this dish into a wholesome and substantial meal, but you can leave it out if you're making an elegant starter.

- 1 cup cracked wheat
- 1 tbsp olive oil
- 6 large ripe figs
- ⅓ cup/1¾ oz pecans
- 4 oz good-quality blue cheese
- 3½ oz arugula
- juice of ½ lemon
- extra virgin olive oil
- salt and freshly ground black pepper

Serves 4

DRESSING SUGGESTION
Classic French vinaigrette
p 183

Place the cracked wheat with 1 tablespoon of olive oil in a pan and heat over low heat. Pour in 1¾ cups water and bring to a boil. Reduce the heat to a simmer, cover with a lid, and cook for 15 minutes or so, until the wheat puffs up. Remove from the heat, separate the grains with a fork, and leave to cool.

Cut the figs into quarters, then, using your hands, break the pecans into pieces. Do the same with the cheese and place everything into a large bowl. Add the arugula and mix together.

Add the lemon juice and some extra virgin olive oil, then carefully add the cracked wheat. Mix thoroughly, season to taste, adding a bit more olive oil if you like, then serve.

GRILLED POUSSIN, SUMAC, ARUGULA, CHICKPEAS, POMEGRANATE

Poussin, or baby chicken, is a great alternative if you don't want to cook a whole chicken. Most butchers have it these days (and can spatchcock it for you), although chicken drumsticks and thighs would be an alternative. We marinate the poussin with sumac and olive oil and then drizzle a bit of pomegranate molasses over the bird once it's cooked. This adds a wonderful sharpness to the smoky grilled meat.

FOR THE POUSSIN

- 4 poussins, spatchcocked
- 1 tbsp sumac
- 4 garlic cloves, crushed
- grated zest of 1 lemon
- Scant ½ cup olive oil
- 4 thyme sprigs
- salt and freshly ground black pepper

FOR THE SALAD

- 3 cups/1 lb 2 oz cooked or canned chickpeas
- 2 scallions, finely sliced
- 2 pomegranates, deseeded
- 1 tbsp olive oil
- 7 oz arugula
- juice of 1 lemon

Continued on page 85

Place the poussin in a large shallow bowl, add the remaining ingredients, except the salt, and turn the poussin until it is coated in the marinade. Cover with plastic wrap and leave to marinate in the refrigerator for 2 to 6 hours.

Meanwhile, in another large bowl, mix the chickpeas, scallions, pomegranate seeds, and olive oil together. Set aside.

Take the poussins out the refrigerator 30 minutes before cooking. Preheat a chargrill pan, griddle pan or barbecue.

Once the poussins have come up to room temperature, place them skin-side down on the hot chargrill or barbecue. After a few minutes, gently begin to lift one of them from the surface: if it moves easily then shift them a little on the grill to brown more of the skin.

When the poussins are well browned on the skin-side, flip them over and either move them to a slightly cooler part of the grill or barbecue and cover with a large lid or put them in an ovenproof pan or dish and place in a hot oven, skin-side up. Cook for another 8 to 10 minutes, or until the poussins are cooked through and the juices run clear when a skewer is inserted into the thickest part of the meat.

- 2 tbsp pomegranate
  molasses
- salt and freshly ground
  black pepper

Serves 4

DRESSING SUGGESTION

Pomegranate dressing p 163

Remove the poussins from the heat, cover loosely with foil and leave them to rest for 5 minutes.

Add the arugula leaves to the rest of the salad ingredients, squeeze the lemon juice over and mix well. Season with salt and pepper and arrange the salad on serving plates.

Cut each bird into 4 pieces, first removing the legs then halving each of the remaining pieces through the center of the breast. Place the pieces on top of the salad and drizzle some extra pomegranate molasses over the whole dish, then serve.

BARBECUED LAMB, EGGPLANTS, BELL PEPPERS, MINT YOGURT, RED CHARD

There is nothing better than a barbecue on a hot day. The lamb is the star of this dish and cutlets are ideal cuts to use on the grill because the meat is very tender when cooked to the right temperature (preferably not over 140°F). It's best served pink and only needs a few minutes cooking on each side.

- 8 rib rack of lamb or 8 lamb cutlets
- 6 baby eggplants
- 1 yellow bell pepper
- 1 red bell pepper
- 1 green bell pepper
- rock salt
- 1-2 tbsp olive oil
- 7 oz red chard
- 1 tbsp extra virgin olive oil
- ⅔ cup/5½ oz Greek-style yogurt
- 1 oz mint, finely chopped
- ½ lemon
- salt and freshly ground black pepper

Serves 4

Preheat a barbecue. Separate the lamb cutlets by slicing in between each bone, or use pre-cut cutlets from the butcher.

Remove the green stalks from the eggplants and cut them lengthwise into halves. Remove the stalks from the peppers and remove the seeds. Cut into equal-sized squares and place the vegetables in a dish together with the lamb cutlets. Season with rock salt and black pepper and drizzle over 1–2 tablespoons olive oil. Put everything on the barbecue grill. Cook, turning frequently. Keep an eye on the lamb, as the fat tends to burn easily and spit.

After about 6 to 8 minutes remove all the vegetables and lamb from the grill. Let the lamb rest on a piece of foil to collect the juices and put the vegetables into a bowl to cool slightly.

Remove the stalks from the red chard, wash if necessary, and roughly chop. Place into a bowl, then season with the extra virgin olive oil and salt. Set aside.

In a bowl, whisk the yogurt with the mint, some salt, pepper, 1 tablespoon olive oil, and 1 tablespoon water to loosen it. Squeeze the lemon over the grilled vegetables and toss them through the chard leaves. Mix until everything is combined.

Arrange the salad on serving plates, adding 2 lamb cutlets per person. Pour any resting juices over the top and serve a dollop of the mint yogurt on top.

SEARED TUNA FILLET, CHERRY TOMATOES, CAPERS, RED ONION, BASIL, CROUTONS

The tomato salad here takes inspiration from a classic Italian dish called panzanella. It's a Tuscan salad with tomato and bread and it's a seasonal mainstay at our stall. We love it with red onion, capers, and basil—it's perfect with fresh tuna, but also good as a little side dish.

- ½ loaf unsliced white bread
- scant ½ cup extra virgin olive oil
- 5½ oz cherry tomatoes
- 1 oz basil, chopped
- 1 tbsp small capers
- ½ red onion, very finely diced
- 2 tbsp red wine vinegar
- 1 tsp sea salt
- 3 red bell peppers
- 4 tuna fillets, about 7 oz each
- 1 tbsp vegetable oil
- salt and freshly ground black pepper

Serves 4

DRESSING SUGGESTION
Basil and arugula pesto
p 160

First, make the panzanella. Preheat the oven to 250°F. Stale bread is best for making croutons. Cut the bread into roughly ½-inch cubes and place on a baking tray. Cook in the oven for about 1 hour, or until the bread is completely dry. Remove from the oven and drizzle the croutons with a little extra virgin olive oil. Season with salt and leave to cool.

Halve the cherry tomatoes and put them in a large bowl with the croutons, basil, capers, and red onion. Pour in the red wine vinegar and olive oil, mix well, add the sea salt, and set aside. The tomatoes need time to macerate and the croutons need to soak up a good deal of the liquid.

Preheat the grill to high. Cut the peppers in half, remove the seeds, and cook skin-side up under the hot grill for about 15 minutes, until they char and soften. Most of the skin will lift away from the peppers, so discard the bits that are easy to remove, but leaving a little gives a nice smoky edge to the flavor. Cut them into bite-sized pieces.

Heat a nonstick skillet over medium-high heat. Season the fish with salt and pepper and brush with a little vegetable oil. Place them into the hot pan and sear each side for about 40 seconds to 1 minute. Don't be tempted to add extra oil to the pan as they will be too difficult to handle and will overcook. When cooked, remove and cut into ¼-inch slices, then arrange on plates with the panzanella and peppers.

OVEN ROASTED RIVER TROUT, NEW POTATOES, CUCUMBER, ROE, SOUR CREAM, DILL

The potato salad in this recipe was inspired by a dish Kristina's mother used to make. In Sweden, fish roe is commonly used and you can find many different varieties in the supermarkets. It adds a lovely saltiness and flavor and works in sauces or as a topping on a shrimp sandwich. The earthiness of new-season potatoes with fresh fish makes for a great combo. Ask your fishmonger to clean and scale the fish before you buy it to save time.

- 1¼ lb new potatoes
- 1 cucumber
- ⅔ cup sour cream
- 3 oz salmon roe
- 1 oz dill, finely chopped
- 2 whole river trouts
- 3 rosemary sprigs
- 2 lemons, 1 lemon sliced
- rock salt
- 2 tbsp extra virgin olive oil
- salt and freshly ground black pepper

Serves 4

Place the potatoes in a large saucepan filled with cold water. Bring to a boil then reduce the heat to a simmer and cook for 12 to 15 minutes, or until they just give when tested with the point of a sharp knife. Drain and set aside: they will continue to soften as they cool.

Cut the cucumber in half lengthwise and scoop out the seeds with a teaspoon and discard. Slice the cucumber into thin diagonal strips.

Put the sour cream into a bowl, then add the cucumber, salmon roe, and dill. Mix well. Slice the potatoes in half and add to the sour cream mixture. Season with salt and pepper to taste. Preheat the oven to 350°F.

Remove the head of the trouts, score them with a sharp knife, and place a sprig of rosemary and a slice of lemon in each score (reserve 1 lemon for later). Season with rock salt and black pepper and brush with half the olive oil. Put the fish on a baking tray and place in the middle of the oven for 20 minutes. Check if the fish is done by inserting a knife into the thickest part of the fish—it should come out hot to touch, and the flesh should be opaque. Once it is ready, remove from the oven and divide the potato salad among serving plates. Place a piece of fish on to each plate, drizzle with the remaining olive oil, and add a lemon wedge.

SMOKED MACKEREL, ROAST BEETROOT, QUINOA, PEA SHOOTS, HORSERADISH CREAM

This is another one of our classic Savage Salads dishes and it's one of the most popular ever among our customers. Horseradish and beetroot work brilliantly together, and the mackerel gives everything a smoky flavor, as well as adding protein together with the quinoa. Quinoa has a lovely nutty taste, but if you want even more nuttiness, throw in some pumpkin seeds or walnuts.

- 2 large beetroots
- 3 cups/1 lb 2 oz quinoa
- ½ tbsp fresh horseradish
- 1 tbsp white wine vinegar
- scant 1 cup heavy cream
- extra virgin olive oil
- 1 tbsp balsamic vinegar
- 1 lb 2 oz smoked mackerel fillets
- squeeze of lemon juice
- 1¾ oz pea shoots
- salt and freshly ground black pepper

Serves 4

Preheat the oven to 350°F. Wrap the beetroots individually in foil, adding 1 tablespoon of water to each, and roast them in the oven for 1½ hours. Remove from the oven but don't unwrap them yet.

Bring scant 3 cups slightly salted water to a boil in a pan. Add the quinoa, return to a boil for a few minutes, then reduce the heat to a simmer, cover, and cook for another 15 minutes, stirring well a couple of times, so the quinoa doesn't catch on the bottom of the pan.

Peel the horseradish then grate it and mix it in a food processor with a pinch of salt and the white wine vinegar. Transfer to a bowl, add the cream, and beat the mixture together until soft peaks form. Season to taste and set aside.

Unwrap and peel the beetroots by hand—the skins should come off quite easily—then cut each in half then into wedges. Mix the beetroot with the quinoa. Add a glug of olive oil and balsamic vinegar, season well, and arrange on serving plates.

Break the mackerel fillets by hand, discarding the skin as you go, and dress the fish with lemon juice and top with pea shoots. Top each plate with the fish and serve with the horseradish cream.

GRILLED CHORIZO, FRESH CORN, BLACK BEANS, AVOCADO, CILANTRO, LIME, SHALLOTS

When sweetcorn is in season it's easy to find and not at all expensive—fresh corn on the cob is much sweeter and crunchier than canned corn and it really makes a difference. You can have this Mexican-inspired dish as a salad, or a tasty filling for a tortilla wrap.

- 3 cups dried black beans (or use canned black beans, drained)
- 4 corn on the cob
- 2 large ripe hass avocados
- 1¼ lb cooking chorizo (about 8 sausages)
- 1 banana shallot, finely chopped
- 1 oz cilantro, chopped
- 1 lime
- extra virgin olive oil
- salt and freshly ground black pepper

Serves 4

DRESSING SUGGESTION
Garlic yogurt p 166

Soak the dried black beans in 8 cups cold water overnight. The next day, drain and rinse then put them into a large pan with 8 cups fresh cold water and bring to a boil. Reduce the heat to a simmer and cook for another 1½ to 2 hours, or until they are soft and almost ready to break apart. Drain, refresh in cold water, and set aside. As a quicker alternative, use canned beans.

Preheat the grill to medium. Remove any stem from each corn cob with a sturdy knife, so that they can easily be held vertically on the counter. Slicing against the corn from top to bottom, carefully cut away the kernels. Bring a pan of salted water to a boil and add the corn kernels. Blanch for 2 minutes, then drain and refresh under cold running water.

Cut the avocados in half then, working your way around the pit, scoop out the flesh and chop into bite-sized pieces.

Score the chorizo. Place under the grill for 10 minutes, or until it sizzles and spits. Alternatively, cook it on a griddle pan until the fat starts to render and it chars.

Place all the ingredients, except the chorizo, lime, and olive oil, in a bowl and mix well. Grate the zest from the lime into the bowl, then cut in half and squeeze the juice in as well. Season to taste with salt and pepper and drizzle olive oil over the top. Divide the salad among serving plates, arranging the cooked chorizo over the top.

WHITE CRAB, CHILLI OIL, AVOCADO, RED ONION, LIME, CHIVES

Unless you're unfamiliar with preparing and cooking a live crab, the best thing to do is buy picked white crab meat from your local fishmonger. This will save you a lot of time and work when making this dish. You can pair this salad with some toasted sourdough, or better yet see if you can get your hands on some Sardinian flatbread (known as pane carasau) from an Italian deli. Or skip the bread altogether and enjoy with a handful of arugula.

- 1 long red chilli, cut lengthwise and deseeded
- scant ½ cup olive oil
- 2 large ripe avocados
- 1 red onion
- 6 chive stalks, finely chopped
- 1 lb 2 oz white crab meat
- 1 lime
- salt

Serves 4

Slice the chilli into fine strips, then bunch the strips together and very finely dice.

Warm the olive oil in a pan over low-medium heat. Add the diced chilli and leave on the heat for about 5 minutes. Be careful not to overheat—you don't want to see the oil bubbling away. Set aside for around 20 minutes, or until the olive oil is infused with some of the heat of the chilli.

Cut the avocados in half, remove the pits, and scoop out the flesh with a spoon before slicing the flesh into about ¼-inch-thick slices.

Chop the red onion finely and put in a bowl together with chives, crabmeat, and avocado slices. Finely grate the zest of the lime into the mixture before squeezing in the lime juice. Season with a little salt and mix everything together.

Serve the salad with a drizzle of the chilli oil on top.

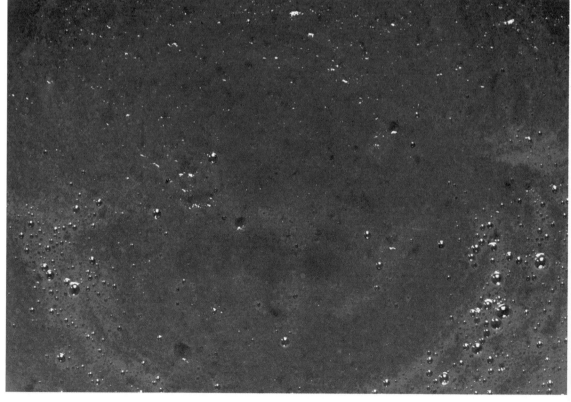

blitzed salad

BEETROOT AND TOMATO GAZPACHO

If you're a fan of traditional gazpacho you should give this one a try. The trick is to use good ingredients including raw beetroot—the pre-packed ones can be preserved in vinegar, so lose their lovely sweet flavor.

- 2¼ lb beetroot
- 2¼ lb vine tomatoes
- 2 celery sticks
- 1 small red onion
- 1 cucumber
- 1 red chilli, finely chopped
- 4 garlic cloves; crushed on the back of a knife
- 2 cups good-quality tomato juice
- 7 oz sturdy, stale bread, such as sourdough
- 2 tsp sherry vinegar
- dash of Tabasco sauce
- scant ½ cup extra virgin olive oil
- sea salt and freshly ground black pepper

Serves 4

Preheat the oven to 425°F. Line an oven tray with foil. Add a little water to the tray, as this will steam the beetroot while roasting. Place the beetroots in the tray, cover with foil, making sure the tray is airtight, and roast in the oven for 2 hours. Roasting the beetroots instead of boiling them will give them a much deeper flavor.

Chop all the remaining vegetables roughly into 2-inch pieces and place on a tray. Add the chilli and garlic and mix well, then season with sea salt. Place in the refrigerator and leave until you are ready to blend all the ingredients together. This will help the vegetables to release some of their juices, resulting in a better flavor.

Test the beetroots with a knife to make sure they are cooked. When done, there should be little resistance. Remove from the oven and leave until cool enough to handle. Peel off the skins and discard, then place them in the refrigerator until completely cool.

When all the vegetables are cool, transfer them to a blender and add the tomato juice, bread, and sherry vinegar. Blend until completely smooth. You can do this in 2 or 3 batches if needed.

Next, strain the mixture through a colander to remove any pulp. Don't use a fine strainer, as we want to retain some of the "body" given by the bread. Aim for a smooth drinkable consistency—add more tomato juice if needed. Season to taste with fine sea salt, ground black pepper, and Tabasco sauce. Finally, whisk in the olive oil until fully incorporated. Refrigerate the gazpacho until completely cold, then serve in chilled glasses.

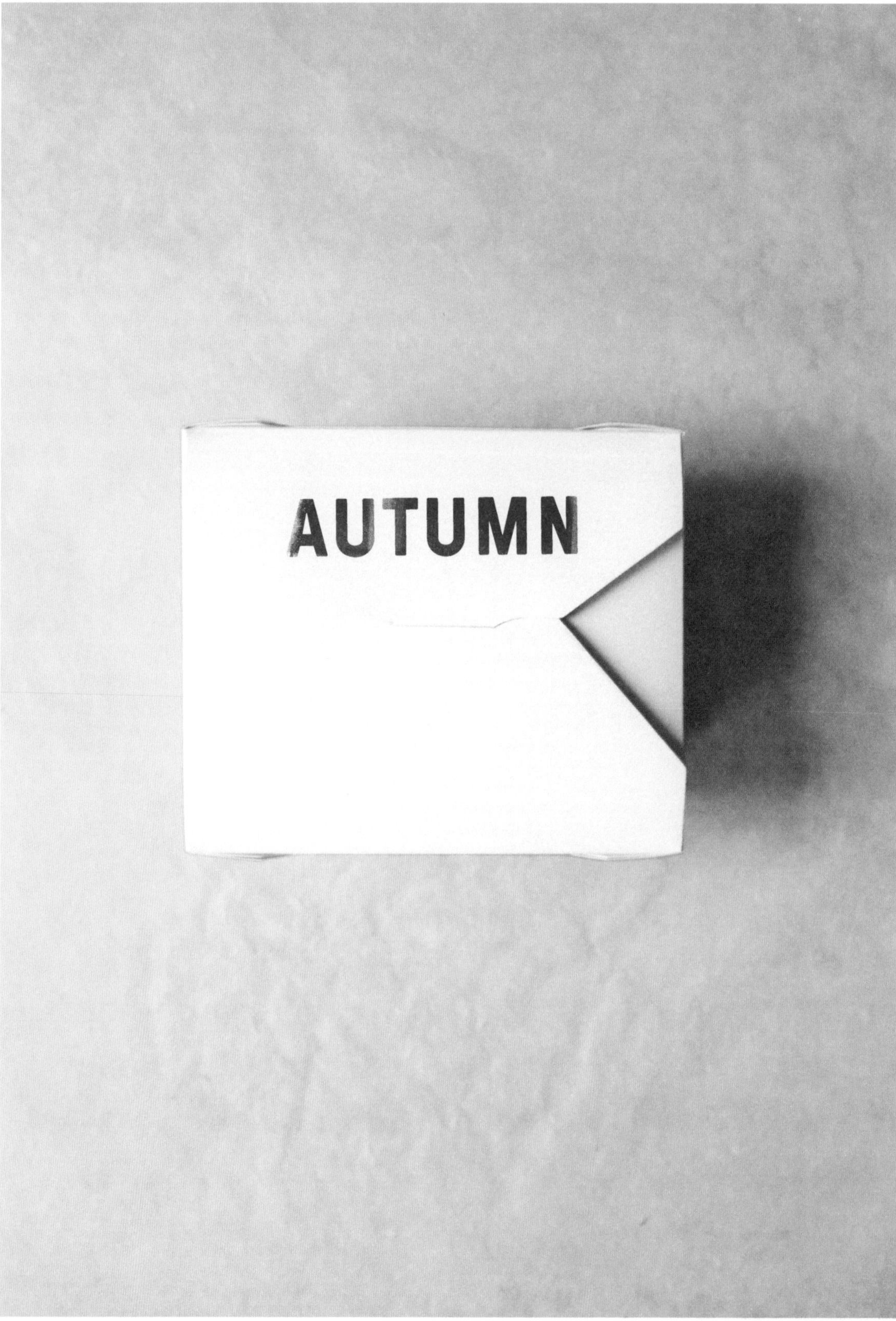
AUTUMN

AUTUMN

Autumn produce is some of the most
substantial and robust you'll get all
year—and it's almost as vibrant as
summer veg. There's orange pumpkin
and sweet potato (the color of
falling leaves), and the piercing
purples of beetroot and red onion.

We use the sweet, earthy flavors of
these bright ingredients combined with
crunchy seeds and satisfying grains and
pulses to create meals that bridge the
gap between light summer dishes and
hearty winter fare, giving you something
nourishing and warming to get stuck into.

If you're creating your own salads, use
your imagination when you choose your
vegetables and try to be playful and
bold when you cook. For example, roast
different-colored beetroots together for
a visually interesting dish, or introduce
a sweet ingredient such as dried fruit.
We know our mushroom and wild rice
salad (page 109) wouldn't be nearly as
interesting if we only used one type of
mushroom, while the roast pumpkin, bulgur
wheat, spinach, and goat cheese salad
(on page 106) is made infinitely better
by the addition of sticky, sweet dates.

FIVE
MINUTE
SALAD

beetroot

kale

apple

pumpkin seeds

sunflower seeds

sherry vinegar

Grate 2 raw, peeled beetroots into a bowl (or cut into matchsticks). Season with salt and pepper and add 1 teaspoon sherry vinegar. Leave the beetroot for 2 minutes to macerate. Chop 10½ oz kale roughly into 1-inch pieces, discarding any thick stalks and stems. Core and quarter 1 apple, then slice thinly into matchsticks. Combine with 1 tablespoon each of sunflower and pumpkin seeds. Add a glug of olive oil and mix well.

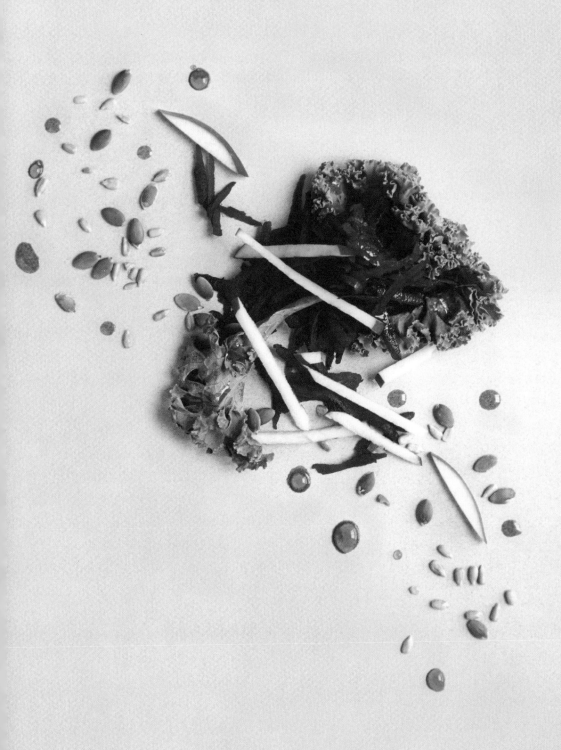

ROAST PUMPKIN, BULGUR WHEAT, DATES, RED ONIONS, SPINACH, GOAT CHEESE

This salad is a number-one hit when the weather begins to turn. It's the ultimate vegetarian salad because it's really hearty and filling. It's delicious both warm and cold, so you can make it in the evening and be the envy of your colleagues at lunch the next day.

- 1 pumpkin, about 2¼–4½ lb
- olive oil, for cooking
- few thyme and rosemary sprigs
- 2 red onions
- 3 cups/1 lb 2 oz bulgur wheat
- juice of 1 lemon
- 1¾ oz dried dates, pitted and quartered lengthwise
- 7 oz spinach
- extra virgin olive oil, for drizzling
- 9 oz soft goat cheese
- salt and freshly ground black pepper

Serves 4

DRESSING SUGGESTION

Orange and honey dressing
p 178

Preheat the oven to 400°F. Cut the pumpkin in half with a large, heavy knife and scoop out all the seeds from the center using a spoon. Discard the seeds (you can toast these to use in another salad). Remove the skin then dice the pumpkin flesh roughly into 1-inch pieces and toss in a baking tray with 1 tablespoon olive oil, salt and pepper, and half the fresh herbs. Roast on the top shelf of the oven for 45 minutes to 1 hour. Use a sharp knife to check when the chunks are soft in the center.

Meanwhile, peel the onions, making sure to leave the root intact (this will help keep the wedges together). Half each one lengthwise, then cut each half into 3 or 4 wedges lengthwise again, through the root.

Place the onion wedges in a baking tray and toss with 1 tablespoon olive oil, salt, pepper, and remaining fresh herbs, then roast in the oven for 30 to 45 minutes. If the onions finish roasting before the pumpkin, put the tray at the bottom of the oven to keep them warm.

Put the bulgur wheat into a heatproof bowl and pour over enough boiling water to cover. Cover and leave for 30 minutes.

When the onions and pumpkin pieces are ready, leave to cool for a few minutes. Separate the bulgur wheat grains with a fork, then dress with a drizzle of olive oil. Season and mix in all the remaining ingredients, except the cheese. Crumble the goat cheese over the top before serving.

SAUTÉED WILD MUSHROOMS, WILD RICE, ROASTED GARLIC, ARUGULA

This dish is inspired by a rice-based salad we created for our stall for the autumn and winter months. It's very easy to make and really tasty and moreish—it's big enough for dinner, and if you make more than you need (and manage to refrain from eating it there and then), it works as a cold lunch the following day. The red rice we use is from the Camargue region in the south of France and has quite a nutty flavor. Its texture is slightly chewy, which makes it the perfect rice to put in a salad. If you can't find Camargue, just substitute for wild rice or simple brown rice.

- extra virgin olive oil
- 1 garlic bulb
- 2½ cups/1 lb 2 oz wild rice
- 14 oz wild mushrooms, such as chanterelles or trompettes de la mort
- knob of butter
- 2 tbsp white wine
- 7 oz arugula
- salt and freshly ground black pepper

Serves 4

DRESSING SUGGESTION
Tarragon dressing p 177

Preheat the oven to 300°F.

Drizzle a little olive oil on the garlic bulb then wrap it in foil and roast in the oven for 30 to 40 minutes. Remove from the oven and leave to cool, then squeeze the garlic from its skin—it should come out quite easily almost as a paste. Discard the skins.

Rinse the rice well under cold running water, then place in a pan, cover with water, add salt, and bring to a boil. Boil for about 30 minutes, or until the grains begin to break up. Drain the cooked rice and set aside. If you're using another type of rice, follow the instructions on the packet.

Prepare the wild mushrooms by brushing off any soil with a small, clean paintbrush, then pick them apart into smaller pieces. Girolles can be split in half by holding the mushroom in both hands from the cap and pulling apart.

The mushrooms need to be cooked quite quickly, so it's important not to overcrowd the pan.

Continued overleaf

To avoid overcrowding, cook the mushrooms in 2 batches. First, heat the butter and a splash of olive oil in a wide skillet over high heat. When hot, add the first batch of mushrooms and move them around a bit so they are coated in oil and butter, then cover with a lid for 30 seconds. Place the cooked mushrooms on to a plate, then repeat with the second batch of mushrooms. Return all the cooked mushrooms quickly to the pan. Add the garlic and white wine and season well with salt and pepper. Continue cooking for another 30 seconds, until all the wine has evaporated.

Pour the mushroom mixture into the wild rice and mix well. Season to taste with salt and pepper, if necessary.

To serve, arrange the salad on serving plates and top with a handful of arugula.

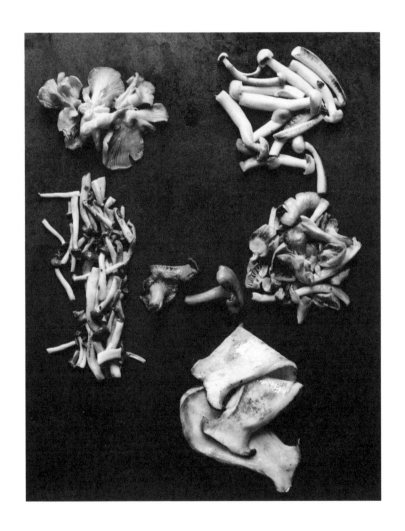

PORK CHOPS, NEW POTATOES, SCALLION, APPLE, WHOLEGRAIN MUSTARD

This potato salad is a lovely plateful, with the sweetness of the apple, the earthiness of the potato, and the sharpness of the mustard and onion all coming together. It's important to make sure you don't overcook the pork chops, as they can go tough and chewy. If you have a meat thermometer, the temperature should be around 158°F for the perfect pork chop.

- 1¾ lb new potatoes
- 1 small bunch of mint
- 4 scallions
- 1 large apple
- 1 tsp wholegrain mustard
- olive oil
- few parsley leaves, chopped
- 4 pork chops
- 1 tbsp vegetable oil
- 2-3 garlic cloves
- few thyme sprigs
- salt and freshly ground black pepper

Serves 4

DRESSING SUGGESTION

Wholegrain mustard dressing p 170

Preheat the oven to 400°F. Boil the new potatoes with the mint in a large pan of salted, boiling water for 12 to 15 minutes, until cooked. Drain and discard the mint. Leave to cool slightly, then cut the potatoes in half and put in a large bowl.

Slice the scallions thinly widthwise. Cut the apple into quarters and remove the core, then cut each quarter into thin slices. Add the apple and scallions to the potatoes, then add the mustard, a glug of olive oil, and the chopped parsley. Season with salt and pepper and mix well.

Pat the pork chops dry with kitchen paper. Using a sharp knife, score the fat side of each chop, cutting through about halfway into the fat, so that they don't warp when cooking.

Heat an ovenproof skillet over medium-high heat. Season the chops with salt and pepper and brush with a little vegetable oil. Add them to the hot skillet with the garlic and thyme sprigs and cook for 3 to 4 minutes on each side, until they become a good golden-brown color. Put the pan in the oven and cook for another 5 to 8 minutes.

Remove from the oven and allow the chops to rest for a few minutes in the pan. Arrange the potato salad on to serving plates with a chop on each one, drizzling the pan juices over the top.

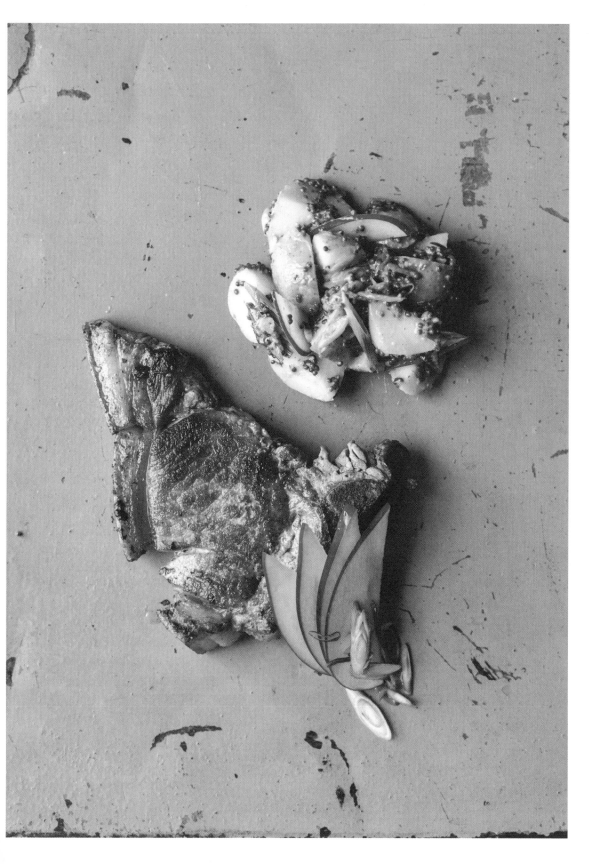

ROAST CAULIFLOWER, BREADCRUMBS, LIMA BEANS, POMEGRANATE, LEMON ZEST

This one is brilliant for vegans—there's protein in the beans, nutrients in the cauliflower and carbs from the breadcrumbs. If you want to add a bit of meat, go for a good quality healthy sausage such as turkey or chicken sausages.

- 3 cups/1 lb 2 oz dried lima beans (or canned lima beans, drained)
- 1 cauliflower
- extra virgin olive oil
- ¼ loaf of stale bread
- grated zest and juice of 1 lemon
- 1 pomegranate
- few parsley leaves, roughly chopped
- salt and freshly ground black pepper

Serves 4

DRESSING SUGGESTION

Citrus dressing p 174

Put the lima beans into a large saucepan, cover with plenty of cold water, and bring to a boil. Once boiling, reduce the heat to a simmer and cook for 1 to 1½ hours, stirring the beans occasionally. Once the beans are tender, drain and rinse under cold running water, discarding any loose bean shells. Alternatively, use canned beans.

Preheat the oven to 400°F. Remove and discard the stem and leaves from the cauliflower, then cut it through the center from top to bottom and cut each half in half again from top to bottom. Make diagonal cuts through most of the stem on each quarter and remove. Next, cut the remaining cauliflower into 1-inch florets, arrange on a baking sheet, drizzle a little oil over, and roast in the oven for 30 to 40 minutes. Remove and set aside.

Reduce the oven temperature to 210°F. Cut the bread into small dice, arrange on a baking tray, and cook in the oven for about 1 hour, or until dry and slightly browned. Remove and leave until cool enough to handle, then break them apart into rough crumbs. Drizzle a little extra virgin olive oil over them and add a pinch of salt and the lemon zest.

Cut the pomegranate into quarters and remove the seeds. Add them to the cooled lima beans with the roasted cauliflower. Dress with extra virgin olive oil and lemon juice, then season well and add the chopped parsley. Arrange on serving plates, sprinkling the toasted breadcrumbs over the top.

SCALLOPS, JERUSALEM ARTICHOKE, CRISPY PROSCIUTTO, CORN SALAD

The marriage of salty prosciutto with the delicate sweetness of scallops is a subtle take on the classic flavor-pairing of pork and seafood. Artichoke is a great root vegetable for soups and purées, but in this recipe we've pan-fried it for a textural twist.

- 1 lb 2 oz jerusalem artichokes
- olive oil
- 5½ oz prosciutto, thinly sliced
- 1 tsp vegetable oil
- 12 scallops, roes removed
- 2 knobs of butter
- 5½ oz corn salad
- juice of ½ lemon
- salt and freshly ground black pepper

Serves 4

DRESSING SUGGESTION
Hazelnut and thyme p 183

Peel the artichokes and cut into ¼-inch slices. Heat a dash of olive oil in a pan over medium-high heat and add the artichoke slices. Fry for 10 to 12 minutes, until they're golden-brown and just start to give when poked with a knife.

Tear each slice of prosciutto into 3 or 4 pieces. Heat a skillet with a little vegetable oil over medium-high heat. Add the prosciutto and very quickly fry them until crisp. Remove and leave to drain on kitchen paper.

Season the scallops with salt and pepper, then drizzle a little olive oil over them and cook in 2 batches (so they don't crowd the pan) in a nonstick skillet (don't add extra oil) for 4 to 5 minutes. You are looking for a golden-brown and light crust to form on the surface.

Cook them lightly; they should reach a warm but not hot temperature in the center. When almost done, add a knob of butter to the pan, and when sizzling, spoon it over the scallops. Remove from the pan and drain on kitchen paper.

Carefully mix the artichokes, corn salad, crispy prosciutto, and a squeeze of lemon juice together in a bowl. Divide among serving plates and arrange 3 scallops on top of each.

ROAST QUAIL, BACON, SPROUTING BROCCOLI, CRUSHED PISTACHIO NUTS, RADICCHIO

Quail is a great alternative to chicken, turkey or grouse. It can be cooked on the bone or deboned. However, as the meat contains very little fat it can easily become dry while cooking. We find cooking the quail wrapped in bacon helps keep the meat succulent and adds a bit of saltiness. The best way to cook it is by roasting it whole in the oven—quick and simple.

- 4 quails, cleaned
- few thyme sprigs
- 8 slices lean bacon
- extra virgin olive oil
- 9 oz sprouting broccoli
- 1 radicchio
- juice of 1 lemon
- 2 tbsp pistachio nuts, crushed
- salt and freshly ground black pepper

Serves 4

DRESSING SUGGESTION
Pomegranate dressing p 163

Preheat the oven to 400°F.

Season the quails inside and out with salt and pepper. Strip the thyme leaves from their stalks and add them to the quails. Wrap each one in 2 rashers of bacon, securing with cocktail sticks, then put into 1–2 large roasting tins. Drizzle with a little oil and roast in the oven for 10 to 12 minutes, turning once. To check if they are cooked, poke one in the thickest part with a thin, sharp knife; the juices should run a pinkish-clear color and the bacon should be sizzling.

Meanwhile, blanch the broccoli in a pan of boiling salted water for 2 minutes, then drain and refresh in cold water.

Cut the radicchio from top to bottom, removing the thick white part, then roughly chop into 2-inch pieces. Place in a bowl, add the broccoli, a squeeze of lemon juice, and a drizzle of olive oil. Toss together.

Season and arrange on serving plates. Top each one with a roast quail, sprinkle over the crushed pistachios, and serve.

GRILLED SQUID, STEWED CHICKPEAS, TOMATO, PAPRIKA, MORCILLA

Most countries have their own take on blood sausages and black pudding and their own ways of serving it. In Sweden, for example, it's pan-fried and eaten with lingonberry jam, while in parts of Italy it's used as a spread on bread. Morcilla is the Spanish variety made with rice and cumin, and it's prized by chefs for its flavor and versatility.

- 3 cups/1 lb 2 oz dried chickpeas (or use canned chickpeas, drained)
- 1 onion
- 1 garlic cloves
- olive oil
- 14 oz can tomatoes
- 1 tsp granulated sugar
- 1 tsp paprika
- 1 thyme sprig
- extra virgin olive oil
- 14 oz squid, cleaned and trimmed
- 7 oz morcilla
- vegetable oil
- grated zest of 1 orange
- few parsley leaves, chopped
- salt and freshly ground black pepper

Serves 4

If using dried chickpeas, soak them in plenty of cold water—at least 2 parts water to 1 part chickpeas—overnight. The next day, drain and rinse in cold water. Put in a large pan, cover with fresh cold water, and bring to a boil, then reduce the heat to a slow rolling boil and cook for 1½ hours, until tender. Drain and set aside the chickpeas.

Chop ¼ of the onion and the garlic clove very finely. Heat a little olive oil in a pan, add the chopped onion and garlic, and sauté briefly for 5 minutes. Add the tomatoes, sugar, paprika, and thyme sprig, then season with salt and pepper and simmer for 30 to 45 minutes. Remove the thyme, transfer to a food processor or blender, and blend until smooth. Mix the tomato sauce and chickpeas together, then check the seasoning and add a dash of extra virgin olive oil. Set aside.

Cut the squid (body and tentacles) into roughly 2-inch pieces, then cut the morcilla into ½-inch circles. Heat a little vegetable oil in a pan over high heat. Season the squid and fry quickly for 4 minutes, until it begins to color. Drop in the morcilla and cook for another 30 seconds, or until the morcilla starts to melt a little.

Serve the squid on top of the chickpeas, spooning the morcilla pieces over the top, then finish by zesting the orange directly on to the plates, and adding a sprinkle of parsley leaves.

DUCK BREAST, GOLDEN RAISINS, ORANGE, RED CABBAGE, KALE, TOASTED ALMONDS

Duck breast is not that commonly used in home cooking, which is a shame because its tenderness and deep flavor can make any meal more sophisticated. Nowadays duck breast can be found in any large supermarket. The cabbage and orange in the salad will really pep up the rich flavors of the duck and makes this a lively meal full of protein.

- 2 large duck breasts
- extra virgin olive oil
- ¼ red cabbage (preferably cut through the root)
- 9 oz kale
- ¼ cup golden raisins
- 2 oranges
- ¼ cup/1¾ oz slivered almonds
- salt and cracked black pepper

Serves 2

DRESSING SUGGESTION

Orange and honey dressing p 178

Preheat the oven to 400°F.

Score the skin of the duck breasts in a criss-cross pattern, about ¼ inch apart. Be careful not to cut all the way through the skin into the flesh. Season with salt and cracked black pepper and rub a little oil on to the skins. Place in a nonstick ovenproof pan skin-side down and cook over medium heat for about 5 minutes, or until the fat of the skin starts to melt. Flip over and sear the flesh side for 2 minutes, then turn back to the skin-side and place the pan in the oven and cook for another 8 to 10 minutes. If your oven is not fan-assisted, place on the upper shelf. The result you are looking for after cooking is a flesh which is not too springy but also not too yielding when pressed with your thumb. It should have an attractive, golden-brown skin. Remove from the oven, cover loosely with foil and leave to rest.

Shred the cabbage finely widthwise until you get to the root (a Japanese mandolin slicer is great for this, but if you don't have one, shred with a knife as finely as possible). Sprinkle a little sea salt over the cabbage—this helps soften the leaves by drawing out some of the water. Discard the root.

Remove the woody, central stalk from the kale leaves. To do this easily, run a pinched finger and thumb from the thinner to the thicker part of the stem to remove the leaves.

Continued overleaf

Discard the stems and cut the leaves roughly into 1-inch pieces. Blanch the leaves in a pan of boiling water for 3 minutes, then drain and refresh in cold water. Drain well.

Place the golden raisins in a small heatproof bowl, pour in a little boiling water, cover, and leave to soak for a few minutes, until they are juicy and plump. Drain and squeeze them slightly by pushing them against the base of the colander. If they are too hot to touch, protect your hand with a clean cloth.

Peel the oranges with a very sharp paring knife, trying to remove as much of the pith as possible, then separate the segments from each other by slicing on either side of the membrane from the outside of the fruit to the inside.

Preheat the grill to medium. Arrange the almonds in a single layer on a baking tray and toast under the grill for about 10 minutes, until they have changed color. Keep an eye on them as they can burn quite quickly.

Place all the ingredients except the duck in a large bowl. Mix well, then season. Slice the duck breasts widthwise at a slight angle from top to bottom and place on top of the salad. Drizzle over the juices from the duck and serve.

blitzed salad

SWEET POTATO, RED LENTIL, AND CHILLI SOUP

This soup is really like a blitzed-up version of one of the salads from our stall. When we make this as a salad, we swap the red lentils for puy lentils and whip up a chilli oil dressing to go with it. The chilli is really what makes this recipe by giving it a great little kick. As a soup, it has a rich and creamy texture (without any cream) and it keeps you full for ages. It's a warming and nourishing soup for a cold autumn evening.

- 1 onion
- 1 celery stick
- 2 garlic cloves
- 1 long thin red chilli
- 1¼ lb sweet potatoes
- 1 tbsp butter
- olive oil
- 1 tsp grated ginger root
- ¾ oz fresh cilantro, leaves only
- 1¼ cups/10½ oz red lentils
- salt and pepper

Serves 4

Chop the onion and celery roughly into ½-inch pieces, then chop the garlic and chilli, discarding the seeds. Peel and dice the sweet potatoes and set aside.

Heat the butter and a splash of olive oil in a large pan over medium heat. When the butter has melted, add the onion, celery, garlic, chilli, and ginger and sauté for 5 minutes. Cover with a lid.

Add the diced sweet potatoes to the pan and cook for another 5 minutes, then add the cilantro stalks and lentils. Increase the heat a little and briskly fry the lentils and vegetables for 2 minutes. You may need to add a little more oil.

Pour in 4 cups water and bring to a boil, then reduce the heat to a simmer and cook for 30 minutes.

Add most of the cilantro leaves (reserve a few for the garnish) to the lentil mixture, then season with salt and pepper. Transfer to a blender in 2 or 3 batches if necessary, and blend until smooth. Be careful as it will be hot. Serve in bowls, garnished with a couple of cilantro leaves.

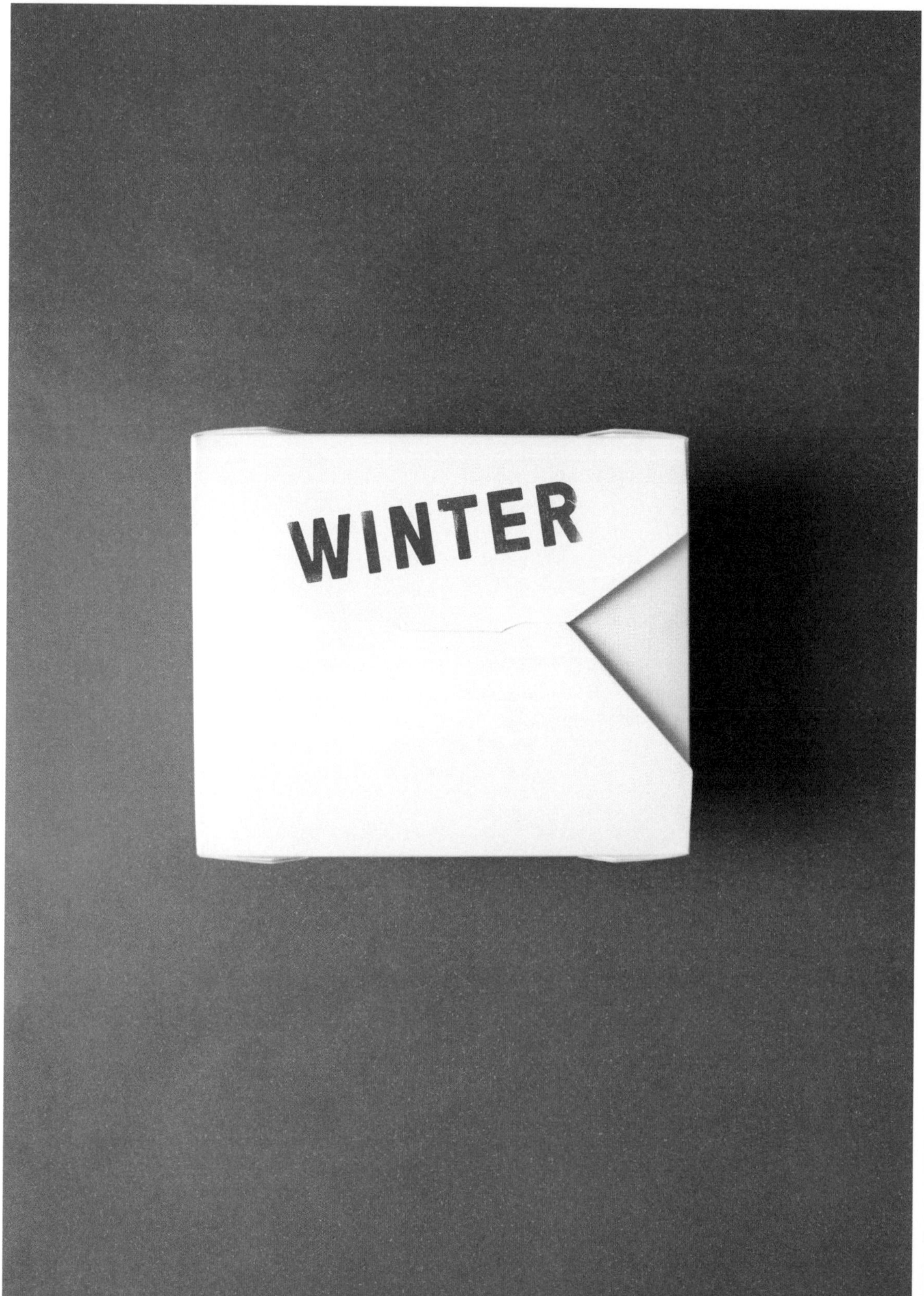
WINTER

WINTER

Winter months are cold, gray, and
dull. Your food, however, can be just
the opposite: warm, colorful, and bold.
Winter vegetables burst with brilliant
hues and rich, exuberant flavors—what
could be more invigorating than tucking
into sweet parsnips, earthy chestnuts,
or fresh brussels sprouts? Winter is
a wonderful time of year to feast
on salads.

Of course, when it's miserable and icy
outside, we seem to crave something
hearty and filling. We want to feel
full and to have enough fuel and energy
to help us cope with the plummeting
temperatures. Salads may not sound like
an obvious solution, but put leafy greens
out of your mind: there are actually
countless vegetable combinations that
are as warming as they are wholesome.

Just look at our lentil, pear, and chicory
salad topped with melting goat cheese (on
page 146). Or turn to the salted brisket,
roasted rutabaga, and pearl barley number
on page 153 for intense flavors and
vivid colors. These are salads that will
brighten even the darkest and dullest of
winter nights.

FIVE MINUTE SALAD

celeriac

walnuts

cornichons

watercress

dijon mustard

mayonnaise

parsley

Grate ½ a peeled celeriac into a bowl, add
the juice of ½ a lemon, and season with salt
and pepper. Break up ¾ cup/2¾ oz walnuts in
your hands, roughly chop 1¾ oz cornichons,
and combine with 5½ oz watercress. For a
dressing, combine 1 teaspoon Dijon mustard,
2 tablespoons mayonnaise, 2 teaspoons
chopped parsley, and a glug of olive oil.
Season with salt, pepper, and a dash of
lemon juice.

GRILLED HALLOUMI, GOLDEN BEETROOT, ORANGE, RED CHARD, WALNUTS

Halloumi is one of the few things we never take off our menu. Traditionally halloumi is made with goat milk, but these days you can find varieties mixed with sheep and cow milk too. There aren't many cheeses in the world that you can put directly on to a grill without it immediately melting, so it's pretty special. In this recipe, the halloumi's rich saltiness marries up perfectly with the sweetness of the beetroot and orange.

- 1¾ lb golden beetroot
- 1 blood orange
- 12 oz halloumi cheese
- extra virgin olive oil
- 5½ oz red chard, thickest part of the stem removed and discarded
- 2 tbsp walnuts, broken
- salt and freshly ground black pepper

Serves 4

DRESSING SUGGESTION

Orange and honey dressing p 178

Preheat the oven to 400°F. Put the beetroot into an oven tray, add a few tablespoons of water, cover tightly with foil, and roast in the hot oven for 1 to 1½ hrs.

To check them, uncover carefully, as the steam will escape very quickly. If they are easy to pierce with a knife they are done. Remove and leave to cool, still covered, for 30 minutes, or until cool enough to handle. Peel off the skins, cut each beetroot in half, then cut each half into 3 or 4 wedges, depending on size.

Peel the blood orange with a very sharp paring knife, trying to remove as much of the pith as possible, then separate the segments from each other by slicing on either side of the membrane from the outside of the fruit to the inside.

Cut the halloumi into ½-inch slices. Heat a little olive oil in a nonstick pan over medium heat. Add the halloumi and fry for 3 to 5 minutes on both sides, until they are browned and the cheese starts to soften.

Place the beetroot, orange, red chard, and walnuts in a bowl, season well and add a dash of olive oil. Mix and arrange on serving plates with the warm halloumi slices on top.

ROASTED ROOT VEGETABLE, TALEGGIO, TARRAGON

Tarragon is a great partner for root vegetables, especially parsnips with their creamy flavor. The taleggio, a semi-soft cheese from Italy, adds depth to this autumn dish. If you can't find taleggio, you can use goat cheese, blue cheese, or camembert. Just don't use these very different cheeses together!

- 4½ lb assorted root vegetable, such as parsnips, carrots, turnips, celeriac
- scant 1 cup peanut oil
- 1 lb 2 oz taleggio cheese
- ½ bunch of tarragon
- 2 tbsp white wine vinegar
- salt and freshly ground black pepper

Serves 4

Prepare all the roots by peeling and chopping roughly into 2-inch pieces. Blanch them in a pan of boiling water for 1 minute, then drain and leave until they are warm, not cool.

Meanwhile, preheat the oven to 400°F.

Put half of the peanut oil in a large tray and heat in the oven. When hot, after about 5 to 10 minutes, add the diced vegetables. Using a spoon, mix them with the oil until they are coated all over. Season with salt and pepper and roast in the oven for about 45 minutes, or until they are golden. Use a slotted spoon to transfer the vegetables to a warm dish.

Remove any skin from the taleggio and break into ½-inch pieces, then set aside.

Blitz the remaining scant ½ cup oil, the tarragon, and the vinegar in a small blender until a smooth dressing is formed. Alternatively, use a stick blender.

Pile the warm vegetables on to serving plates, adding the cheese and dressing as you go, finishing with extra taleggio and a good drizzle of the dressing. If you wish, you can also add a few winter leaves, such as mizuna, to the salad.

PICKLED HERRING, FENNEL, DILL, CUCUMBER, DRIED CRANBERRIES, DARK RYE

Pickling your own herring involves a bit of planning ahead, but if you have the time it's well worth it. In Sweden pickled herring is included at every traditional buffet table and comes in all different styles. The Savage Salads way is to include it as part of a fresh and crunchy salad with cranberries, which add a powerful and fruity punch.

- 1⅓ cup rock salt
- 1 cup granulated sugar
- ½ tsp black peppercorns
- 1 thyme sprig
- rind of 1 lemon
- 10½ oz fresh herring fillets

FOR THE PICKLING LIQUOR

- 2 cups white wine vinegar
- ¼ cup granulated sugar
- ½ tsp black peppercorns
- ½ bunch of dill

FOR THE SALAD

- 1¼ cup dried cranberries
- 1 fennel bulb
- ½ cucumber

Continued on page 140

Prepare the herring fillets a day in advance. Mix the rock salt, sugar, half the peppercorns, thyme, and lemon rind together in a bowl until all the ingredients are evenly mixed. Spread half of the mix over the base of a small-medium dish.

Pat the herring fillets dry with kitchen paper and lay them on top of the salt and sugar curing mix. Cover with the remaining cure. Cover the dish with plastic wrap and chill for 12 hours.

To prepare the pickling liquor, heat scant ½ cup of the vinegar, the sugar, and the remaining peppercorns in a small saucepan over low heat until the sugar has dissolved.

Pour in the remaining vinegar and scant ½ cup cold water and add the dill. Transfer to a bowl, cover with plastic wrap, and chill in the refrigerator until completely cool.

Remove the herring fillets from the curing mix and rinse under cold running water to remove any excess cure.

Pat dry with kitchen paper, place into the pickling liquid, and leave in the refrigerator for 12 hours.

- 2 tbsp extra virgin olive oil
- juice of ¼ lemon
- salt and freshly ground black pepper
- dill, to garnish
- 4 slices dark rye bread, to serve

Serves 4

DRESSING SUGGESTION

Use a little of the pickling juice

For the salad, put the cranberries in a small heatproof bowl, cover with lukewarm water, and leave to soak for about 1 hour until they resemble semi-dried raisins.

Shred the fennel bulb as finely as possibly, cutting against the grain (a Japanese mandolin slicer is perfect for this, otherwise, use a very sharp kitchen knife). Slice the cucumber in the same way, cutting widthwise into circles. Drain the cranberries and, using your hand, gently squeeze out any excess water and place in a large bowl.

Place the fennel and cucumber in the bowl and dress with olive oil and lemon juice. Season with salt and pepper.

Arrange the salad on serving plates, then divide the herring fillets between them, placing them on top of the salad. Garnish with dill and serve with rye bread.

VENISON CARPACCIO, PICKLED MUSHROOMS, CAULIFLOWER, BROCCOLI, BABY SORREL

Venison is a wonderfully succulent but lean meat, full of flavor and therefore perfect when prepared as carpaccio. Carpaccio is a classic Italian dish made with raw meat, most commonly beef. You should always use a tender cut, such as a loin, with very little fat. Pickles are great companions to a carpaccio, as some sharp piquancy is welcome as a counterpoint to the meat.

- 1 lb 2 oz venison fillet
- ½ tsp cilantro seeds
- 1 cup white wine vinegar
- 1 garlic clove
- 1 thyme sprig
- a generous pinch of salt
- 2 tsp granulated sugar
- ½ head broccoli, cut into small florets
- ½ head cauliflower, cut into small florets
- 9 oz mix of small mushrooms, such as enoki and bunashimeji
- 3½ oz baby sorrel
- extra virgin olive oil

Serves 4

Trim any remaining fat from the venison and cut into very thin slices. Place the meat between 2 sheets of plastic wrap and, using a meat mallet, gently bash the meat to make it slightly thinner. Be careful not to break it as it will be delicate. Set aside in the refrigerator.

Heat the cilantro seeds gently in a large dry pan for 5 minutes, or until they are aromatic. Add the vinegar, garlic, thyme, salt, and sugar, then bring to a boil. Add the broccoli, cauliflower, and mushrooms, return to a boil, pour in scant ½ cup cold water, and remove the pan from the heat.

Remove the venison from the refrigerator. Leaving the meat wrapped in the plastic wrap, slice it very thinly. Arrange the sorrel on the serving plates. Unwrap the venison and arrange on top, sprinkling the pickled vegetables over the meat. Finish with a drizzle of extra virgin olive oil.

GRILLED SIRLOIN, ENDIVE, GUINNESS CARAMELIZED RED ONION, BLUE CHEESE

Sirloin is a fantastic cut of beef from the back of the animal. The bitterness of the endive, the strong blue cheese, and the sweetness from the caramelized red onion makes a great combination together with the beef. The Guinness adds a bit of smoky quality to the sweet onions—and you can always enjoy what is left in the can while cooking!

- 1 large red onion
- extra virgin olive oil
- scant ½ cup Guinness
- 1 thyme sprig
- 1 tsp balsamic vinegar
- 4 sirloin steaks, about 7-9 oz each
- 2 heads endive
- 7 oz stilton cheese
- salt and freshly ground black pepper

Serves 4

DRESSING SUGGESTION
Tarragon dressing p 177

Slice the onion quite thinly. Heat a little olive oil in a pan over medium-high heat and add the onion. Cook for 5 to 10 minutes, until it softens. Add the Guinness, thyme leaves, and balsamic vinegar and season with salt and pepper. Increase the heat to high and continue to cook until all the liquid has evaporated. Remove the pan from the heat and leave to cool.

Preheat a griddle pan or grill. Season the steaks well and cook on a hot griddle pan or under the grill until cooked to your preference: 3 to 4 minutes on each side for rare and 5 minutes on each side for medium-rare. Remove and leave to rest.

Chop the endive roughly into 1-inch pieces, discarding the dense part at the root.

Crumble the blue cheese into a bowl with the endive. Add the cooled red onions and mix well. Add a dash of olive oil and arrange on serving plates with the sliced steak on top.

WARM GOAT CHEESE, LENTILS, PEAR, GOLDEN RAISINS, CHICORY

This is a great vegetarian winter salad. There are many varieties of goat cheese, but when baking it in the oven this way, the best one to use is a chèvre type, as it has a rind around it holding it together. Always make sure that your oven is fully preheated before putting the cheese in so that it gets good color quickly and doesn't melt completely.

- 14 oz puy lentils
- 14 oz cups firm goat cheese
- extra virgin olive oil
- 2 ripe pears
- ⅓ cup golden raisins
- 1 bulb chicory
- few flat-leaf parsley leaves
- salt and freshly ground black pepper

Serves 4

DRESSING SUGGESTION
Classic French vinaigrette
p 183

Put the lentils in a large pan, cover with plenty of water, bring to a boil, and cook for 10 to 15 minutes, or until they are just soft. Drain and rinse under hot running water.

Preheat the grill to medium-high. Keep the goat cheese rounds whole, or if using a large round to share, cut the goat cheese into ½-inch slices and place on a baking sheet. Drizzle with a little olive oil and add a twist of black pepper then cook under the grill for 5 to 8 minutes, until browned.

Cut each pear lengthwise into 8 pieces, removing the core from each piece as you go.

Roughly chop the chicory, discarding the dense part at the root end, and place in a bowl with all the ingredients except the cheese. Drizzle a little olive oil over and mix well.

Arrange the salad on serving plates with the warm goat cheese on top.

CRISPY PANCETTA, CANNELLINI BEANS, BRUSSELS SPROUTS, PRUNES

Brussels sprouts are often completely forgotten outside of Christmas, but with a little imagination they can stand proud in salad dishes on any winter day. Here they're served with pancetta, beans and prunes: a better use for sprouts than as a sidekick to turkey!

- 1¾ cups/10½ oz dried cannellini beans (or use canned cannellini beans, drained)
- 9 oz pancetta, thinly sliced
- 9 oz brussels sprouts
- 5½ oz semi-dried prunes
- olive oil
- 1 tsp red wine vinegar
- salt and freshly ground black pepper

Serves 4

DRESSING SUGGESTION
Basil-infused oil p 178

If using dried, put the cannellini beans in a large bowl, cover with plenty of water, and leave to soak overnight. The next day, drain the beans, then place in a large pan and cover with plenty of fresh water. Add 1 teaspoon of salt and bring to a boil. Once boiling, reduce the heat and simmer for 30 minutes, checking occasionally to make sure there is still enough water covering the beans. Once the beans are tender, drain and rinse under cold running water, then set aside.

Preheat the oven to 325°F. Line an oven tray with parchment paper. Arrange the pancetta slices on the parchment, place another sheet of parchment on the top, then place another tray on top so that the slices remain completely flat. Cook in the oven for about 15 minutes, checking a couple of times to see if the pancetta is becoming darker and slightly rigid, and remove some of the melted fat. Carefully remove the slices from the tray and leave to drain on kitchen paper.

Cook the sprouts in a pan of boiling salted water for 8 to 10 minutes, or until just soft. Drain and leave to cool slightly, then cut each in half.

Roughly chop the prunes and mix in a bowl with the cannellini beans, halved sprouts, a pinch of salt and pepper, a drizzle of olive oil, and the red wine vinegar.

Spoon the salad on to serving plates and arrange a few slices of the crisp pancetta on top. Try with the basil-infused oil on page 178.

LAMB, SWEET POTATO, TURNIP, CRISPY KALE, SESAME SEEDS

Many cuts of lamb can be quite fatty, but in this recipe we use fillet from the loin which is one of the leanest cuts. It's great for sliding on to skewers for a Mediterranean and Middle Eastern touch.

- 3 garlic cloves
- grated zest of 1 lemon, juice of ½
- 1 bunch of rosemary, roughly chopped
- olive oil
- 2¼ lb lamb loin fillets
- 1¼ lb turnips
- 1¼ lb sweet potatoes
- 7 oz kale, trimmed
- 1 tbsp sesame seeds
- salt and freshly ground black pepper

Serves 4

DRESSING SUGGESTION
Garlic yogurt p 166

Crush the garlic and grind into a paste with a pinch of salt in a mortar and pestle. Put into a bowl with the lemon zest, chopped rosemary, a twist of pepper, and a glug of olive oil. Dice the lamb fillets into 1½-inch pieces, add to the bowl, and mix well, pressing the marinade into the lamb. Cover and leave in the refrigerator for 2 hours.

Meanwhile, preheat the oven to 350°F. Peel and dice the turnips and sweet potatoes into 1-inch pieces. Place in a roasting tin, drizzle with olive oil, season with salt and pepper, and roast in the oven for 30 to 40 minutes.

Blanch the kale in a pan of boiling water for 30 seconds, then drain and refresh in cold water. Drain again and dry well. Arrange the kale in a single layer in an oven tray, season with a little salt, drizzle with olive oil, and mix well with your hands until the kale is coated all over. Cook in the oven for 5 to 10 minutes. Remove and leave to cool.

Toast the sesame seeds in a dry nonstick skillet over low-medium heat for 10 minutes or so, tossing them occasionally to make sure they don't burn. Set aside.

Preheat the grill or barbecue. Thread the lamb pieces on to metal skewers. Season with salt and cook either under the grill or preferably on a barbecue, turning them frequently, for 8 minutes for medium and 12 to 15 minutes for well done.

In a bowl, mix the cooked turnips, sweet potatoes, and sesame seeds together. Add the kale and check the seasoning. Divide the salad among serving plates and add the lamb skewers.

SALTED BRISKET, HONEY ROASTED RUTABAGA, PEARL BARLEY, CAVOLO NERO, PARSNIP CRISP

Salt beef is meat that has been cured in salted water. It's an easy but long process that can take up to two weeks to become ready. We offer a relatively fast and easy version in this recipe: you can find it pre-salted in shops or from a Jewish butcher.

- 2¼ lb piece salt beef, uncooked
- 1 large carrot
- 1 celery stalk
- 1 onion
- 1 garlic bulb
- 1 tsp black peppercorns
- few thyme sprigs
- 2 bay leaves
- 1¼ lb rutabaga
- 1 tbsp honey
- olive oil
- 2⅓ cups/1 lb 2 oz pearl barley
- 1 head of cavolo nero
- 2 parsnips
- vegetable oil
- juice of ½ lemon
- salt and freshly ground black pepper

Serves 4

Place the salt beef in a large saucepan, cover with cold water, bring to a boil, and then remove from the heat. Discard the water, clean the pan, and return the salt beef to the pan. Add the carrot, celery, onion, garlic, peppercorns, thyme, and bay leaves. Once boiling, reduce the heat to a very gentle rolling boil and cook for about 3 hours, topping up with water if necessary.

When ready, the meat should come apart quite easily when pulled with a fork. Remove the pan from the heat and leave to rest in the cooking liquor until ready to serve.

Preheat the oven to 350°F. Peel and dice the rutabaga roughly into 1½-inch pieces and blanch in a pan of boiling salted water for a few minutes, then drain. Whisk the honey with roughly equal the amount of olive oil together in a bowl or pitcher and use to dress the rutabaga. Place the rutabaga in a roasting tray, season with salt and pepper and roast in the oven for 20 to 30 minutes.

Put the pearl barley into a pan and cover with the broth from the salt beef—check that it's not too salty. If it is, add some fresh cold water. (If using the broth, then set some aside for drizzling over the salt beef at the end.) Bring to a boil and cook for about 15 minutes, then drain.

Continued overleaf

DRESSING SUGGESTION

Salsa verde p 168

Prepare the cavolo nero by separating the leaves from each other and removing the thickest part of the central stem of each leaf. Cut the remaining leaves into roughly 2-inch pieces and blanch in a pan of boiling salted water for 3 to 5 minutes. Drain and refresh under cold running water then drain again.

Peel the parsnips, discard the skin, and continue to work with the peeler, cutting it into thin strips.

Pour 2 inches of vegetable oil into a large deep saucepan and heat over medium-high heat until the oil reaches 350–400°F when tested with a cooking thermometer.

Carefully add the parsnip strips in batches and deep-fry until golden-brown. Move them around in the oil with a metal slotted spoon, so they cook evenly. As soon as they are golden-brown, remove them with the slotted spoon and drain on kitchen paper.

Mix the rutabaga, cavolo nero, and pearl barley together in a large bowl. Add a squeeze of lemon and season to taste. Divide the salad among serving plates.

Remove the salt beef from the pan, cut into thick slices, and add them to each plate, glazing each pile with a little of the salt beef broth. Top each one with a few parsnip crisps and serve.

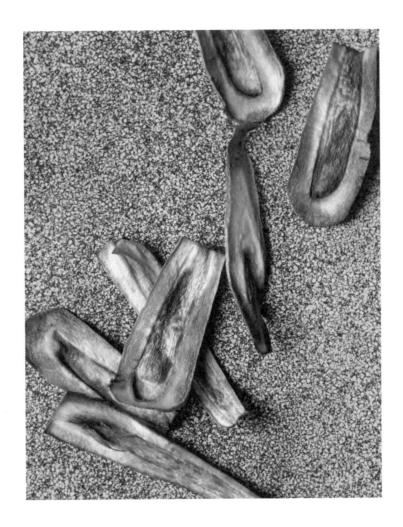

blitzed salad

CABBAGE SOUP WITH ALMOND OIL

A good winter soup should be comforting and rich, but it needn't be laden with calories. Cabbage soup is known as a mainstay for dieters and those on a health kick because it's low in calories and high in fiber. We fortify ours with chicken broth to add a bit of extra flavor. For a heartier option you can add potatoes and cream. Topping with a drizzle of almond oil gives an elegant finish.

- 1 tbsp butter
- 3½ oz mild white onion, finely chopped
- 1 garlic clove
- 1 celery stalk, peeled
- 1¼ lb green cabbage (any variety), chopped
- 3½ cups chicken broth
- 1 thyme sprig
- almond oil or good-quality hazelnut or extra virgin olive oil, for drizzling
- salt and freshly ground black pepper

Serves 4

Heat the butter in a large saucepan over low heat. When melted, add the onion, garlic, and celery. Cover with a lid and gently sweat for about 10 minutes. Add the cabbage, increase the heat slightly, and sauté, stirring constantly, for 2 minutes.

Add the chicken broth and thyme, bring to a boil, then reduce to a simmer and cook for another 10 minutes. Take out the thyme and remove the pan from the heat.

Transfer the mixture to a blender, in 2 or 3 batches if necessary, and purée until completely smooth. Be careful as the mixture is hot. Check the seasoning, pour into a pan if it has cooled too much and reheat gently until warm.

Serve in bowls with a drizzle of almond oil over the top.

DRESSINGS AND DIPS

BASIL AND ARUGULA PESTO

This is our take on the classic basil pesto with the addition of arugula for a lovely peppery taste. The best way to make this is to roughly chop everything by hand rather than blitzing it all in a blender. Make sure you add the arugula (and keep tasting) as you go along, as some types are more peppery than others and it can easily overpower the basil. It's quick and easy to make and tastes a lot better than the ones you buy in a jar. If you have any left over, cover it with olive oil and put in the refrigerator—it will keep for a week.

- 2 tbsp/¾ oz pine nuts
- 1 oz arugula
- 1 oz basil
- 2 tbsp/1 oz parmesan, grated
- 1 garlic clove
- 6 tbsp extra virgin olive oil
- salt and freshly ground black pepper

Approx 4 servings

Toast the pine nuts in a dry skillet over low heat for 5 to 10 minutes, turning the nuts frequently until they are golden-brown. Remove the pan from the heat.

Chop all the dry ingredients very finely, including the toasted pine nuts, then place in a bowl and mix together with the olive oil.

Grate in the parmesan and season to taste.

BLACK OLIVE TAPENADE

Tapenade is a dip or spread that comes from Provence in France. When you make a tapenade it's important to use top-quality olives and a good olive oil. We usually use kalamata olives, as their fruity flavor makes a brilliant base. This gives a salty punch to the mild flavors of white fish or chicken.

Blitz all the ingredients together in a food processor. Alternatively, chop the olives, capers, and parsley very finely with a sharp knife and place in a bowl. Whisk in the olive oil and lemon juice until everything is combined.

- 1 cup/7 oz black olives, pitted
- 1 tsp capers
- few parsley leaves, chopped
- 4 tbsp extra virgin olive oil
- juice of ½ lemon

Approx 4 servings

POMEGRANATE DRESSING

The sweet tang of pomegranate vinaigrette is an interesting accompaniment to both meat and fish.

In a bowl, whisk together the olive oil and pomegranate molasses. Add the vinegar and whisk again. Season to taste with salt.

- 4 tbsp olive oil
- scant ¼ cup pomegranate molasses
- 1 tbsp red wine vinegar
- salt

Approx 4 servings

SPICY ROMANO RED PEPPER PESTO

We absolutely love this pepper pesto and have served it at several events as a dip or part of a buffet. It's delicious as a topping on bread or as a complement to chicken or white fish. We prefer using romano peppers as they are a little sweeter than the usual bell peppers, and we've added a bit of chilli to give it some heat—it's just as lovely with or without it.

- 1 red romano pepper, halved and deseeded
- 1 red chilli, deseeded and finely chopped
- 1 garlic clove, finely chopped
- 1 tbsp grated parmesan
- 6 tbsp extra virgin olive oil
- pinch of salt

Approx 4 servings

Preheat the oven to 400°F.

Place the pepper halves on a baking tray and roast in the oven for 20 to 30 minutes, or until the skin turns black and starts to blister. Remove from the oven and leave to cool slightly.

Peel the skin off and discard.

Chop the pepper finely, place in a bowl, and add the remaining ingredients. Mix together until combined.

LEMON AND DILL DRESSING

These two ingredients have been cozying up to fish dishes for decades—this dressing is all you need to take your seafood salad to the next level.

Whisk all the ingredients together in a bowl.

- scant ¼ cup lemon juice
- ⅔ cup extra virgin olive oil
- 1 tsp chopped fresh dill
- pinch of salt and freshly ground black pepper

Approx 4 servings

GARLIC YOGURT

This yogurt dressing provides a light alternative to a classic and much-loved condiment—aioli.

Pound the garlic and salt together in a mortar with a pestle until combined. Alternatively, very finely chop the garlic and salt with a heavy knife, then place in a bowl, add the remaining ingredients, and whisk together until combined.

- 1 garlic clove
- pinch of salt
- scant 1 cup/7 oz Greek yogurt
- 2 tbsp water
- 1 tbsp extra virgin olive oil

Approx 4 servings

SALSA VERDE

An Italian classic meaning "green sauce". There are many ways to make a salsa verde but the key ingredients are the green herbs. Most commonly you add olive oil and white vinegar, but you can also add anchovies, capers, mustard, shallots, or anything else you fancy—depending on what you want to serve it with. It goes well with fish, meat, or vegetables, and we often use is as a dressing in potato salads.

Chop all the dry ingredients together with a sharp knife, then put into a bowl. Whisk in the olive oil and white wine vinegar until combined.

Check the seasoning, adding a pinch of salt if it is needed.

- 1 tbsp capers
- 10 basil leaves
- ⅓ oz mint leaves
- ⅓ oz flat parsley leaves
- 1 small garlic clove
- 1 anchovy fillet
- 6 tbsp extra virgin olive oil
- 1 tsp white wine vinegar
- salt

Approx 4 servings

SHERRY VINAIGRETTE

One for colder days: sherry vinaigrette is rich and warming. It also acts as a great base to other dressings.

Whisk all the ingredients together in a bowl until combined.

- 1 banana shallot, very finely chopped
- scant ½ cup sherry vinegar
- scant 1 cup extra virgin olive oil
- pinch of salt

Approx 4 servings

WHOLEGRAIN MUSTARD DRESSING

Another classic—hot, and perfect with pork.

In a bowl, slowly whisk the peanut oil into the mustard until it is a thick emulsion. Whisk in the vinegar, then slowly whisk in the olive oil until all the oil has been used. Whisk in scant ¼ cup water and season with salt and pepper to taste.

- scant ½ cup peanut oil
- 1 tsp wholegrain mustard
- scant ¼ cup white wine vinegar
- scant ½ cup olive oil
- salt and freshly ground black pepper

Approx 4 servings

SMOKED PAPRIKA AND LIME HUMMUS

Making your own hummus is simple and quick. There's no cooking involved and you only need a handful of ingredients. The key is getting the balance of the ingredients right. Here we've swapped the lemon juice for lime and added smoked paprika for some spice.

Drain the chickpeas and reserve the water. Blend all the ingredients together in a food processor, adding a little of the reserved water from the chickpeas to loosen. Season to taste with salt.

- 14 oz can chickpeas
- grated zest and juice of 2 limes
- 1¾ oz tahini paste
- 1 tbsp extra virgin olive oil
- ½ tsp smoked paprika
- 1 garlic clove
- salt

Approx 4 servings

BLUE CHEESE DRESSING

This is particularly effective at lifting leafy salads with its deeply savory flavors. It's also delicious as a dip.

Blend all the ingredients together in a food processor, seasoning to taste if necessary.

- 1¾ oz strong blue cheese
- scant ¼ cup crème fraîche
- 1 tsp white wine vinegar
- 1 tbsp extra virgin olive oil
- pinch of garlic powder
- pinch of superfine sugar
- salt and freshly ground black pepper

Approx 4 servings

CITRUS DRESSING

Citrus is a classic base for dressings. It's simple but ideal in fruity salads or served with fish. Use orange, grapefruit, or lime instead of lemon for an unusual twist.

Whisk all the ingredients together in a bowl until combined.

- scant ¼ cup lemon juice
- ⅔ cup/5 fl oz extra virgin olive oil
- pinch of salt and pepper

Approx 4 servings

WATERCRESS MAYONNAISE

Watercress has one of the strongest flavors of any salad leaf and delivers a welcome peppery edge here.

Put the egg yolks and mustard in a bowl together with a few drops of the oil and beat. Then, very slowly at first, whisk the remaining oil into the emulsion until you are halfway through the oil. Add the white wine vinegar and continue whisking in the oil until it is used up. Set aside.

Blanch the watercress in a pan of boiling water for 10 seconds, then drain and add to the mayonnaise. Transfer the mayonnaise to a food processor and process until it is puréed. Season to taste.

- 2 egg yolks
- 1 tsp Dijon mustard
- 1¼ cups peanut oil
- 1 tsp white wine vinegar
- 5½ oz watercress
- salt and freshly ground black pepper

Approx 4 servings

TARRAGON DRESSING

The sweet aniseed tones of tarragon are a good match for root vegetables. Too much can be overpowering, so using it in a dressing helps strike a beautiful balance.

Whisk all the ingredients together in a bowl until combined. Leave to infuse for at least 30 minutes before serving.

- 1 banana shallot, very finely chopped
- scant ½ cup sherry vinegar
- scant 1 cup extra virgin olive oil
- 1 tbsp chopped tarragon
- pinch of salt

Approx 4 servings

ORANGE AND HONEY DRESSING

Sweet and sticky, this one is best when on top of warm meat salads and roasted veg.

- 1¾ cups orange juice
- 1 tbsp honey
- grated zest of 1 orange
- salt

Approx 4 servings

Bring three-quarters of the orange juice to a boil in a pan and cook until it has reduced by three-quarters. Add the remaining orange juice together with the honey and mix the zest into it.

For a bolder flavor, peel the orange and slice into very fine strips (julienne). Season to taste with salt.

BASIL-INFUSED OIL

Strong aromatic herbs like basil are ideal for mixing with olive oil to create flavorful dressings that last for weeks. This recipe also works with sage.

- 1¾ oz basil or sage leaves
- 1¼ cups extra virgin olive oil

Approx 4 servings

Put the herbs in a bowl or pitcher, pour in the oil, and leave to steep for a minimum of 24 hours. Use this oil to drizzle on to your favorite salads.

GINGER AND SESAME DRESSING

For a taste of those bracing Asian flavors, ginger and sesame can't be beaten. This hot, nutty dressing will add depth and excitement to any salad.

Whisk all the ingredients together in a bowl until combined.

- 1 tbsp grated ginger root
- 1 tbsp sesame oil
- 1 tbsp lemon juice
- salt and freshly ground black pepper

Approx 4 servings

COCONUT YOGURT

This is a taste of the tropical. Coconut yogurt works well as a creamy accompaniment to chicken salads.

Whisk all the ingredients together in a bowl until combined. Season to taste with salt.

- 5 tbsp coconut milk
- 1 cup/9 oz Greek yogurt
- 1 tbsp extra virgin olive oil
- salt

Approx 4 servings

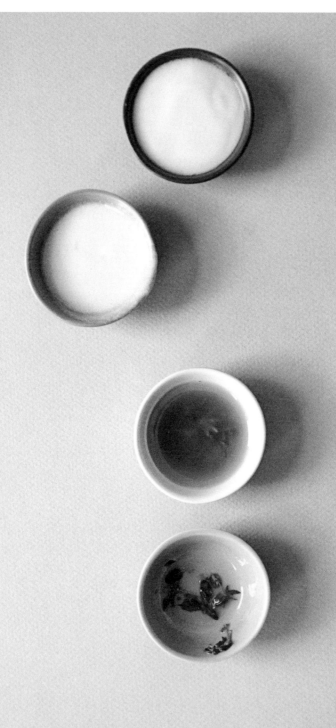

HAZELNUT AND THYME DRESSING

This nut and herb combo is best with a chicken salad.

- ⅓ cup/1¾ oz hazelnuts
- 1 tbsp thyme leaves, chopped finely
- 1 tbsp sherry vinegar
- scant ½ cup peanut oil
- scant ½ cup extra virgin olive oil
- salt and pepper

Approx 4 servings

Gently toast the hazelnuts in a dry skillet over low heat for 10 to 15 minutes, until golden-brown. Remove from the heat and leave to cool slightly before breaking them into smaller pieces with a pestle and mortar or chopping with a heavy knife.

Whisk all the ingredients together in a bowl, then season to taste with salt and pepper.

CLASSIC FRENCH VINAIGRETTE

- scant ½ cup peanut oil
- 1 tsp dijon mustard
- 2 fl oz/scant ¼ cup white wine vinegar
- scant ½ cup olive oil
- salt and black pepper

Approx 4 servings

Slowly whisk the peanut oil into the mustard until it is a thick emulsion. Whisk in the vinegar, then slowly whisk in the olive oil until it is all used. Whisk in scant ¼ cup water and season with salt and pepper to taste.

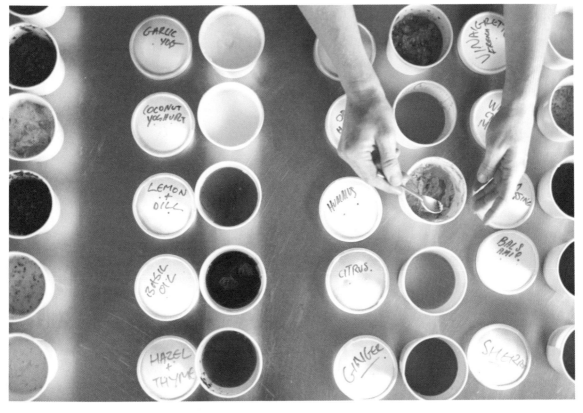

INDEX

THANK YOUS

Savage Salads (Kristina and Davide) would like to say a big thanks to our commissioning editor Zena Alkayat and our agent Marigold Atkey—thank you for believing in us, without you this book would not have happened. We would also like to thank Charles Bell who has been a huge help in the making of this book.

Thanks to Kim Lightbody for the beautiful photography and to Marente van der Valk for the brilliant styling. Thanks also to Kathy Steer and Hilary Bird.

Finally we would like to thank our parents Kerstin, Stiggan, Maria Teresa, and Domenico, as well as our brothers and sisters Anders, Ingrid, and Lisa, and our partners and friends Irene, Karla, Nagaite, Sumeia, Andrea. Thank you all for your endless support and help over the years.